"For years I have wondered, how ca[...] is so spiritual be left in the hands of [...] their book *Colorful Connections: 12 Questions About Race That Open Healthy Conversations*, Dr. Saundra Dalton-Smith and Lori Stanley Roeleveld take the issue of race and, with incredible wisdom and surgical precision, bring together all of the different dynamics and weave them into a balanced, biblical solution. I can say with certainty that this book is the way forward!"

ISAAC PITRE, president of II Kings Global Network and IPM Ministries, and author of *The Divine DNA*

"Saundra and Lori have done a masterful job stepping into a vital subject. Their wisdom, wit, candor, and grace can help each reader explore and grow in themselves and their relationships. Thanks to both of these wonderful women for giving us such a timely and helpful resource!"

SARAH BOWLING, founder of Living Genuine Love, founder of Saving Moses, author, speaker, and TV host

"If you only read one book this year, make it this one! Authors Dalton-Smith and Roeleveld have done a masterful job of helping us to face important issues. Their invitation to join the conversation about race, ethnicity, justice, disagreement, and differences will challenge you to move in the direction of positive change. *Colorful Connections* will give you the tools to make a lasting impact on the racial relationships of future generations."

CAROL KENT, speaker, founder and executive director of Speak Up Conference, and author of *When I Lay My Isaac Down*

"I'm so proud of Saundra and Lori for unapologetically and straightforwardly tackling such a crucial subject. Just when it seems we have made little progress over the decades, here comes *Colorful Connections* offering more than mere hope. These women offer unblinking advice and model strategy that goes way beyond wishful thinking. They open a door to authentic cross-cultural friendships that lead to true understanding."

JERRY B. JENKINS, novelist, biographer, and founder of
The Jerry Jenkins Writers Guild

DR. SAUNDRA DALTON-SMITH
AND LORI STANLEY ROELEVELD

12 QUESTIONS ABOUT RACE THAT
OPEN HEALTHY CONVERSATIONS

KREGEL
PUBLICATIONS

We dedicate this book to everyone
trying to be part of the solution.

Cataloging-in-Publication Data is available from the Library of Congress.

ISBN 978-0-8254-4735-8, print
ISBN 978-0-8254-7790-4, epub
ISBN 978-0-8254-6942-8, Kindle

Printed in the United States of America
22 23 24 25 26 27 28 29 30 31 / 5 4 3 2 1

Contents

To Our Readers

BEFORE WE BEGIN THIS conversation, we want you to know that we are just like many of you. We love Jesus Christ. We believe his Word and seek to apply it to every aspect of our lives. We struggle. We're imperfect. When we fail, we try again.

Saundra is a wife, mother, doctor, writer, speaker, Southerner, and black woman. Lori is a wife, mother, grandmother, crisis worker, writer, speaker, Northerner, and white woman. But of course, like you, we are also each much more than our roles, geography, and skin color.

Within these pages there are also voices of men and women of other ethnicities adding their thoughts to ours. Together we are the body of Christ, sons and daughters of the Most High King.

We have been impacted, just like you, by the events and debates about race and ethnicity raging in our times. We aren't experts at racial reconciliation, but because we are writers, that's what we offer to God in the work toward racial healing. We committed to have this public conversation in writing in the hope that it would inspire other Christians to begin (or continue) their own conversations.

We did this because we love Jesus and believe that, in him, we have the power and the love we need to heal and move forward together. We did this because we believe God when he says we need one another and that we are one body. We did this even though it was uncomfortable, scary, and made us vulnerable. We offer this work to you with love, tears, and prayers.

As hard as it is to hold on to hope for change in our times, we believe we have every reason to hope in Christ. May this book ignite, reignite, or further fuel your hope as well, in the name of Jesus.

—Mercy and grace, Saundra and Lori

How to Get the Most from This Book

Lori

You may not have planned to read a book about racial conflict and healing. Saundra and I never planned to write one. But here we all are, by God's grace.

In our customary modes, Saundra writes and speaks about the value of sacred rest and freedom in Christ. I write about persisting in faith and having hard conversations. But through several incidents we describe in the book, God invited both of us into this written conversation. Our hope is that this book will encourage you to initiate your own conversations and make colorful connections.

When Saundra and I started this project, we were acquainted with one another, but we weren't close. We were friendly, but we weren't friends. We'd encountered one another at writing conferences, were aware of each other's work, even shared a literary agent, but besides admiring her writing, I didn't know if she had a family, where she lived, or what church she attended for worship.

We both approached this project with a desire to use our gifts to make a difference, to move closer to racial healing. We initially experienced fear, but we elevated our fear of the Lord above all other fears and agreed to have a transparent, public conversation on race, not knowing what we would encounter from one another.

Once we agreed to try this, we met face-to-face virtually and discussed ground rules for our work. We weren't working in the dark with these ground rules. I'm experienced at having hard conversations and leading individuals and groups through them. These are guidelines I've tested in my personal life, work life, and church life. Now, Saundra and I are testing them here in a new arena.

We each initiated certain chapters, and we responded to each other's specific questions without "pre-discussing" them. We just wrote and sent the raw material on to the other writer. That was scary, but it most closely mimics the conversations we're encouraging everyone to have. There was an advantage in that we'd be exploring this topic as we got to know one another. That is precisely the situation with many of you, making new connections and entering this conversation with people you don't know well.

Like you, we faced our own fears on this project; you will see glimpses of this along the way. Saundra responded to the project with a gutsy enthusiasm that inspired and frightened me at the same time. She had immediate ideas about transparent modeling, open dialogue, and being hard to offend, which made me believe we could do this.

In one of our first conversations about ground rules, I blurted out one of my many concerns. "We have such a shared vision for this project, I'm half afraid we'll have to work through disagreements along the way and half afraid we won't, and the book won't be of any use."

She responded with unhesitating confidence, "Oh, don't worry. We'll have disagreements."

I gulped and asked God to supply me with courage moving forward. I plowed ahead for these reasons:

First, God opposes the proud, and I desire to cultivate a humble spirit. As my blind spots, prejudices, and wrong thinking are exposed through this conversation, it will provide more fuel in my spiritual battle against pride. As uncomfortable as that is, humility pleases God.

To love is to listen.

Second, while like many of my friends, I don't believe that I'm a racist, I do believe I have much to learn about brothers and sisters of color and their experience of Jesus, the church, and life on this planet. I'm confident there are ways I can grow and change to be a better representative of Christ in their lives and to demonstrate love in ways that are meaningful to them. I trust that God will use this process to show me attitudes and sinful mindsets I won't see if I don't bring my thoughts into the light.

Third, to love is to listen. Part of our ministry as believers is to witness one another's lives and, in love, listen to one another's stories. I want to hear Saundra's experience as a Jesus-loving woman of color living and raising sons in the South. I want to be present with her and hard to offend out of love for her. I want to lay down my self-defensiveness the way Jesus laid down his life.

Listening is one step forward we can all take. One simple way we can be part of the solution. I'm also excited that Saundra is willing to listen in love to what it's like to be Christian and white in these times of racial tensions. If she and I can help to alleviate fears and open doors for others to have these conversations, then I want to present myself for the challenge and trust God to help me rise to it.

What you'll see in the following chapters is the dialogue Saundra and I had in writing, wherein we discussed twelve questions leading to twelve steps every Christian can take toward racial healing. We created ground rules for our conversation that you'll find toward the end of the book. There's a reason for presenting them there. Saundra will explain.

Saundra

It may seem odd to present the seven keys for hard conversations in the next to last chapter of this book. Let me share with you some of the reasoning behind this decision. Let's look at treating bias, stereotypes, and prejudice in the same way one would approach treating a medical problem. How can you develop a medicine to treat an illness if you do not know what brought it on in the first place? If you don't know the foundation for the problem, it's impossible to treat the core issues at the heart of the problem. Only then can you develop solutions with the potential for long-term healing and transformation.

*We must not fear exposing the biases and
prejudices we harbor in our hearts.*

When Lori and I started our conversations, key areas we addressed were the biases and stereotypes we believed. In my research during the process of writing this book, this is always shown as a needed first step. We must not fear exposing the biases and prejudices we harbor in our hearts. Bringing them into the light is part of the healing process. This requires vulnerable and honest self-reflection. And it causes you to answer the question: Do I associate negative qualities to specific groups of people?

From here you are then able to reflect on why you may have an easier time associating with certain groups of people but struggle with building relationships with others. Being aware of your own biases does not mean you should feel bad or see yourself as a bad person. Rather than making you feel condemned, it should instead raise awareness of these issues and motivate you to address them. Stereotyping is a learned behavior, and as with any behavior, it can be unlearned with the renewing of our minds. This is the hope we have for overcoming hatred, injustice, and prejudice. What has been carried over through past generations and the current cultural climate can be redeemed when minds are aligned with the mind of Christ.

In a study on how to reduce prejudice, it was found that after the initial awareness to the problem, the next phase is cultivating concern.[1] When we care about the outcome, we are more likely to become engaged in being a part of the process. We move out of apathy into participation. We become part of the solution.

We encourage you to read the book on your own or to invite a friend or small group along for the journey. Each chapter begins with the questions we asked one another and that we challenge you to ask. Then Lori and I respond. This will sometimes feel like you're listening in on our conversation, but that is our way of keeping this real for us all.

Then, following our dialogue, you'll read how another person of a different ethnicity responded to the topic of that chapter. Finally, each chapter ends with a practical step we can all take, Scripture to consider, and starting places for taking action.

When doing this with a group, we recommend asking the following five questions for every chapter. We've also included additional discussion questions specific to each chapter at the end of the book.

Five Questions to Ask for Every Chapter

1. What resonated with you most about what Saundra or Lori shared? What sparked the most response from you? With what did you agree or disagree? How has your experience been either similar to or different from what each of them shared?
2. How would you respond to the primary question being asked in this chapter?
3. What are your thoughts on how the Bible passages mentioned relate to the topic of this chapter? What other passages would you consider in exploring this question?
4. What would you like people in your discussion group to know about you regarding the topic of this chapter?
5. What do you see as your next step in responding to this chapter?

You've likely chosen this book because, like us, your desire is to serve God and to be part of his ministry of reconciliation. We are not experts in this but we serve a God who is, so we move forward in faith that he is with us. "If God is for us, who can be against us" (Romans 8:31), yes?

Chapter One

COMMIT TO THE CONVERSATION

IT'S HARD TO KNOW where to begin.

They say the first step is always the hardest, and that's never been truer in our times than in conversations about race, color, and ethnicity. Most Christians feel a desire and a biblical mandate to be part of a healing process and to engage in the ministry of reconciliation in these conversations. Many of us are convinced of God's love of diversity, and we long to cultivate it in our relationships, congregations, and communities. But where do we begin?

We suggest that you begin the same place we did. First, we each explored our "why." Why would we do this? Why put ourselves out there with each other? Why put ourselves out there in front of readers? Why take the risk of exposing ourselves, of pushing past fear, and of opening ourselves up for possible hurt? Once we answered our why, we committed to engage in a conversation about color, ethnicity, and race.

You, our reader, will also explore *your* why and consider making the commitment to engage in conversation. Knowing our why helps us keep talking even when it gets hard. Making the commitment keeps us accountable before God and one another to see the conversation through.

In this chapter, we each tell the story behind why we chose to commit to having a conversation about race and ethnicity. At the end, you'll have opportunity to explore your why and also to commit to engage in the conversation.

But first, it's important to define terms so we all have a clear understanding of what exactly is being discussed. Biblically, we don't believe there is more than one race. We recognize and celebrate variations in skin color, countries of origin, and cultural ethnicity, but we only recognize one race—humanity. However, in modern vernacular, *race* is a term often used as a synonym for skin color, ethnicity, or nationality. For clarification in our book, we will most often refer to ethnicity or skin color, but for ease of communication, we may also use the word *race*. When we use the term *racist* or *racism*, we are referring to the practice of judging or discriminating against someone based on their skin color, nationality, or ethnicity.

WHY ENGAGE IN CONVERSATIONS ABOUT RACE AND ETHNICITY?

Saundra

"Did you see the video?"

I didn't have to ask my son which video. There was no need for further clarification. We had all seen what can only be described as an inhumane way to die.

Regardless of the man's innocence or guilt. Regardless of what you do or don't believe about the person in authority inflicting the pain. You could not unhear the sounds of distress as he pleaded for his life. You could not detach yourself from the cries of the onlookers trying to negotiate assistance for someone they saw in trouble. This was not a Hollywood movie scene, where we could all walk away at the end of the show and know everyone was safe, healthy, and at peace. No, this was real life.

And for the first time, my brown-skinned son was an eyewitness to what it can look like to live in a world where prejudice can be fatal.

"I can't understand why someone would do that to another human being. Why would anyone do that?" he asked.

There are questions for which there are no answers or at least no satisfying answers. There is a time to share further with him the realities of prejudice and injustice in our world. There is a time to elaborate on the history of all those who have paved a way before him, a time to educate him on the life of black and brown people that his school textbooks fail to disclose. There is a time to share with him my concerns about how this may affect him in the future, so he is not blindsided if one day he comes face-to-face with injustice and discrimination. But then there is also a time to comfort in the moment until the pain of what has just been experienced has lessened enough for us to be able to move forward into a place of healing.

"I don't know. I just don't know," I replied honestly as I wrapped my arms around my now-taller-than-I-am child and hugged him a little tighter than I had the day before.

There are things that a mother expects to worry about when thinking about the future of her children. Will they choose the right college? Will they make good decisions around their friends? Will they marry someone who loves God? Will they honor their wedding vows and raise a family? These are concerns that come with parenting, regardless of skin color. Red or yellow, black or white, we want our kids to have the best opportunities and the ability to have a good life.

And then there are the situations you worry about when your child has dark eyes, dark hair, and deeply pigmented skin. Concerns like—will people see him for who he truly is or will they stop with the outward observation, make a judgment call, and then act on their own biases rather than from a place of truth? Will the color of his skin be the deciding factor rather than his ability or his character?

Over the ensuing month, these were the thoughts that stood out most in my mind. Prayers for my children's spiritual growth and the maturing of their faith alongside prayers that they would be treated justly. Prayers for them to experience and be given the same opportunities as those in the majority.

These feelings did not present for the first time during that wave of racial unrest, although the news of fresh violence and oppression did bring them to the forefront. Those emotions have been present from the first time I stared down into the big brown eyes of my firstborn son. From the moment I realized I had the privilege and the responsibility to aid in the development and equipping of a brown-skinned boy in a culture rooted in a history of prejudice against those who look like him.

When I see new stories of racial injustice in the media, it reawakens a hard reality about the current state of equality. It reminds me of the chasm that yet remains and the great need for racial healing. It mocks my hoped-for improvement in society and taunts me to stop believing in the possibility of reconciliation. Despite experiencing my own past moments of prejudice, a part of me dares to believe things have changed. Certainly my children won't have to navigate the same terrain I did forty years ago. Right? But it seems the current climate is not in agreement with my desires and prayers.

Racial tension peaks and abates throughout each year, depending on the political scene, reported mistreatment, and recorded violence directed toward black and brown people. Each escalation comes to a pinnacle whenever there is a death.

Thousands take to the streets in protests. Some with a desire to peacefully gather to show solidarity and support. Others with the desire to unleash the anger and frustration accrued over years of feeling marginalized. Both trying to process pain. One doing so in a way that has the potential to build bridges, while the other in a way that generally only results in further damage. Damage to communities, damage to morale, and damage to the potential of changing the views of those who are actively displaying prejudice and bias.

I have never considered providing any type of training on what is prejudice, bias, or discrimination. I'm often perplexed by the request of well-meaning white friends to share my tips on how they can be more inclusive. It seems unusual for the one experiencing the injustice to be the one called to educate those perpetuating it. Yet, this was what I noticed in the days following news of another black person killed during an arrest, or jogging down the street, or sitting in her home, or while wearing a hoodie. Overnight my blackness makes me an expert in all things race-related. Let me assure you, this is not the case. I am not an expert in diversity, inclusion, or equality training. There are many experts with excellent resources that I recommend you check out at the back of this book.

What I am is a black woman who sits every Sunday on a church pew surrounded by people of every race. We worship together and it's a beautiful sound. The lilting highs of the sopranos are balanced by the deep undertones of the altos as we join in declaring, "Lord, you're holy." The diversity creating a synthesis that is harmonious and echoes the voice of heaven.

It's a sound some churches have been able to enjoy within their four walls but have found challenging to take outside those same walls into their communities. It's a sound other bodies of believers have yet to experience because the faces filling the pews all look alike—lovers of Jesus whose places of worship still look like the segregated '60s, void of any signs of inclusion and absent the unity they profess.

Just in case you didn't catch this the first time, let me repeat it for those in the back pew: I am not an expert on race relations. What I am is a follower of Jesus, degreed, and trained in studying the body, mind, and spirit. I thrive on learning what makes people do what they do, feel what they feel, and act how they act.

I'm also a black mama who is tired of being afraid for my black children growing up in a world where their blackness is counted against them even before they open their mouths to demonstrate their intelligence and gifting.

Above all, I'm a woman who looks at what I see possible on Sunday morning at my church during times of worship and wonders why we can't take that same harmony of diversity out into the world. What would it look like to invite others into our experiences? What can we each do to be an ally to those of another race? What melody would arise out of the church and infuse the culture if we began to treat every occasion like a choral production? Where we look for the diversity that is missing but needed to birth a fuller sound within our relationships, our businesses, and our homes?

The body of Christ should be of one spirit, but we come in an array of beautifully colored packaging, complete with different personalities, talents, and skill sets. It's impossible to expect those who do not know God to effectively practice equality and inclusion when those who proclaim to know him don't know how to practice it.

As a business professional, I've found many Christians who are willing to mentally join arms with me to take the kingdom of God and the message of Jesus out into the marketplace. But those same people forget that the kingdom is one of diversity when the time comes to pick the ones with whom they will physically join arms. The result is conferences where everyone is of one race.

Creating diversity and inclusion is an intentional process of loving another as yourself.

Sometimes there is a feeble attempt at allyship with a 90:10 ratio of majority to minority representation. Having one person of color on a board or on a stage is not diversity; it is an insult. Creating diversity and inclusion is an intentional process of loving another as yourself. It's making room at the table for someone who has never even been invited into the room. It's working toward a balance of representation so that everyone can see themselves in those standing on the platform.

When I was initially asked to participate in this writing project, my first thought was *Absolutely not! I'm not going to put my thoughts out there.* Race is not a subject the church does well, and I had no desire to get pulled into the dysfunction.

To make it more stressful, I didn't know Lori well enough to be sure we could have a real conversation about race without ending up hurting each other in the end. Before I could hammer out a quick email reply, I knew the reasons I had for not wanting to participate were the very reasons to do it.

Many of us shy away from conversations on race. We fear we won't know what to say or that we will say it wrong. In our avoidance, we keep putting bandages on a festering wound. We act like the world is color-blind. It's not, and I don't want it to be. I want to live in a world that is color aware.

Maya Angelou said it best in her poem, "Phenomenal Woman." I want you to see my brown skin, full lips, and thick hips and not judge me any differently than a woman with white skin. I want you to be aware of the diversity I bring to a conversation due to the experiences I've had as a black woman. I don't want you to be blind to the diversity I bring. I want you to embrace it.

I joined Lori on this journey to walk through the process of having a conversation on race with another woman who doesn't look like me, who hasn't experienced what I've experienced, and who isn't someone with whom I hang around. We had been friends on social media for years, liking posts and cheering each other on in our writing careers, but we had never discussed deep things. She knew nothing about the details of my life. In fact, we had only met in person on a few occasions. We've shared a single meal together around a table of fellow authors with our mutual agent. We've come to this project as two women who have nothing to bind us together other than faith. The core thing we have in common is loving Jesus. At the beginning, I couldn't help but wonder: Will that be enough?

Can we bring our differences to the table and talk about hard things without taking offense? Can we share our raw emotions on racism, cancel culture, and life for minorities in America and do so in a way that respects the feelings of the other? Because this is the conversation that needs to happen in every church, every boardroom, and around our dinner tables. This is where healing begins, one-on-one. Neighbor to neighbor. Colleague to colleague. It's an internal process of binding up wounds, prejudices, and biases of individual hearts to create a foundation on which we can stand rooted in love, unity, and righteousness.

My prayer for this project is for the Holy Spirit to guide us through these hard conversations on race and to bring us out on the other side with more love, joy, peace, patience, kindness, goodness, faithfulness, gentleness, and self-control. I believe he can do this and so much more when we come with open hearts and willing spirits. Let the conversation begin.

Lori

I stood in a national chain store accused of trying to pass three counterfeit fifty-dollar bills.

It was an uncomfortable, embarrassing experience that Sunday afternoon when the register clerk flagged the manager and asked me to step aside. The lines were long. Everyone stared as they held my bills to the light, gestured for store security, and eyed me suspiciously.

Security asked to open my bags. Awkwardly I endured strangers pawing through the undergarments I was attempting to buy with the cash my mother had slipped into my Christmas card. I trembled when asked to move into the office. They called the police.

By God's grace, I could use my bank card to cover the purchase. Uniformed officers arrived and questioned me about the origins of the suspect fifties. They recorded my answers and allowed me to leave, warning that the secret service would contact me. Outside, I fell apart.

But I walked away.

The manager was firm but calm, believing the bills were counterfeit but not quite viewing me as "someone trying to pass a bill." The police were respectful. And while the situation was excruciating, I never once imagined it wouldn't be worked out. Not for one second did I fear for my life.

Days later, the secret service informed me my bills weren't counterfeit. I could retrieve them from headquarters. "Store staff make this mistake all the time," he said.

Nightly, I see stories of other Americans suspected of wrongdoing—passing a counterfeit twenty, driving a possibly stolen vehicle, or running through a neighborhood where a break-in has occurred—that don't end like my story did.

The details differ. I was a middle-aged woman with no arrest history buying underwear in a small town. Some incidents involve people with arrest histories. Some occur in cities plagued with unrest—citizens on edge. Some suspects respond calmly and co-operatively; others resist, argue, or run.

Still, there's one distinction that stands out. I'm white. The people in the headlines are often black. If my skin had been the color of theirs, would I have been afforded the benefit of the doubt or would the conversation have been relocated to the police station?

Did the way I responded make the difference, or did my expectation of fairness, respect, and reason impact the way I responded? Was it simply a matter of geography (I live in Rhode Island, not the South or in a major city) or a dynamic of ancestry because I descend from an Anglo-ethnic mix of Irish/English/French? Would a woman of color have been afforded the same respect? Would she have a story to tell, or might she have become a story on the evening news?

While I don't believe racism lurks within every white person, I believe there is sufficient statistical and anecdotal evidence to support the contention that prejudice and bias still impact people of color on multiple levels in our times.

That said, I never planned to write about racism.

Maybe, like me, you've never planned to talk about racism. Maybe, like me, you've used some of the same reasoning to watch from the sidelines rather than engage directly in the work. As I share what's held me back, consider what may have factored into your own hesitation.

We all have something to contribute to the conversation about racism, but it is wise, loving, and biblical to listen first.

As a white woman, I'm not anyone's first choice to hear from on this issue. What could I possibly have to contribute? Perhaps you've wondered the same thing. The message I take from the reigning voices of the day is that this is my time to be quiet, listen, and make space for voices that have not, historically, been heard. And there is truth there, but it's not the whole truth. We all have something to contribute to the conversation about racism, but it is wise, loving, and biblical to listen first.

Also, I've reasoned with myself, the church of Christ is a body with many parts. None of us individually is called to do every task assigned to God's people. Individuals have a variety of callings, so no individual bears all the work. In the past, I trusted that some are called to be vocal activists in the war against racial hatred. Maybe, like me, you've wished you were one of them. While we work to eradicate hatred in our own hearts and raise our children to love others, we aren't sure what other action to take. So perhaps, we decide, tackling racism is "someone else's job."

Looking back, I wonder if the choices I made were because I wasn't sure what to do or if it was just because it wasn't easy. Worse, I wonder if I would have made different choices if my children's lives depended on it. That's a factor in this conversation, isn't it? That by virtue of skin color, some of us consider racial reconciliation an elective of the faith, not a required course. Like many of you, I wasn't consciously trying to disengage or avoid this conversation, I just didn't think I had the credentials to speak, and I didn't readily see the on-ramp for me to join. But it also wasn't a problem that stared me in the face every day or impacted my children's lives on a regular basis. If it had, I believe I'd have worked harder to find that on-ramp.

My worldview, shared by many Christians, contributes to my dilemma regarding what form involvement takes. Biblically, we don't believe there is more than one race. We recognize and celebrate variations in skin color, countries of origin, and cultural ethnicity, but we only recognize one race—humanity. Try bringing that up in an unnuanced conversation. But now I see that rather than using that as justification for remaining silent, I should seek out and/or create opportunities for nuanced conversations.

Many of us oppose what we call racism but see it as a manifestation of hate stemming from fear, ignorance, selfishness, and disordered values. Racism, ethnicism, and hatred are sins. Sin can't be educated out of a person, protested out of a community, or legislated out of a society (although those actions have their roles). Humanity's sin was addressed on the cross of Jesus, and it is there that every individual must go to become free of it.

So rather than write about race, I continue to write about Jesus.

Many of us read and understand some accusers' indictments of the church, but in our thinking, not everyone calling themselves Christian is a follower of Christ. We dismiss some of this criticism because we suspect that those perpetrating the harshest narratives are only posing as believers. When people complain about racist believers, we consider the phrase an oxymoron. Racism, as is true of all hatred, cannot coexist with the Holy Spirit of Jesus Christ.

Admittedly, some Christians have come out of racist backgrounds and repented of this sin but still fight old mindsets. I also imagine Christians of every skin color may be tempted to hate, to yield to prejudicial stereotypes, to suspect ill of others who are different from them. But no one who embraces hatred or prejudice can rightly consider themselves to be walking in step with the Spirit of Jesus Christ.

So we invest in evangelism, discipleship, and biblical teaching about spiritual growth, trusting that others see this as our contribution to eliminating racism in the church. But while we approach the situation indirectly, those who are directly impacted by racism feel unheard, undervalued, and sometimes unloved.

This should not be, and it means our approach is insufficient for our times.

We need to be agents that cross divides and ease tension. That is a calling given to every believer.

Are we only concerned with the most extreme forms of racism? Do we not want to root out any form of division that might take root in the church? Do we not want to stretch ourselves to love one another the best we can in every way we can? We need to be willing to admit that there is more to this conversation than simply denying we are racist, and be willing to seek God's strength and power for change. We need to be agents that cross divides and ease tension. That is a calling given to every believer.

But we all have excuses. Have you ever felt as if you'd like to contribute to ending racism, but your reach seemed too small, your gifts and skills felt irrelevant and inadequate, and even your location seemed to make it a challenge to make any contribution of worth? Those are the times we need to remember how much God can do with what little we offer. The lesson of the loaves and fishes is relevant to our struggle in committing to invest what little we have to offer in the face of such an extensive and widespread conversation.

I certainly don't say this from a lofty perch of "I've always done it right." There was a long time when I believed I wasn't called to write about racism, and I tried to "stay in my lane"—writing about Christ. This wasn't because I didn't believe firmly in treating others with respect and love. I think mostly it was because I wasn't seeing racism in my direct experience.

But then, after a summer of explosive headline events, one of my blog readers emailed a simple request: "Lori, we need you to write a post sharing your wisdom on how to have the hard conversation about race. Hope to read it this week."

He follows my writing and referenced my book *The Art of Hard Conversations*. I care about meeting the needs of my readers and have considerable experience with hard conversations, so, at last, my on-ramp appeared. Here was something I could contribute to this conversation—guidelines about how to have hard conversations about race.

Several blog posts followed, one of which would eventually become the outline for this book. Still, the Holy Spirit, readers, godly friends, and an editor challenged me to go further. Did I have the courage to have and document a hard conversation with a black author? Was I willing not only to instruct about hard conversations but to have an authentic one publicly?

I don't know. Was I?

That sounds like a great idea, but again, here I am a middle-aged white woman with no significant track record of ministry in this area. I believe the right things, but where I live, that's seldom put to the test. Still, that makes me like many other white Christians who want to be part of the solution but don't know where to begin. I decided that perhaps I could make a worthwhile contribution in this way. It's one thing to string words together in a clever post; it's quite another to make myself vulnerable to another Christian with the plan of allowing others to see my missteps, questions, blind spots, and revealed sins.

We know from Psalm 139:15 that God knew each of us when we were being formed and we know from Acts 17:26 that he chose this time and place for us to live. We know from 2 Peter 1:3 that he has provided everything we need for life and godliness. Whether we feel like it or not, we have all we need to enter this conversation and to do this work. The hardest step is the first one.

You see, I am afraid of what others will think of me, of discovering in front of people that I have places to repent and change. And, like many other Christians, my greater fears are missing out on all God has for me in Jesus Christ and of leaving any of what he's given me unused in the work to which he's called me. I know many of you would also list this as your greater concern, and that's why you've picked this book up and made a commitment to consider having this conversation.

As I wrote this chapter, I thought about the parable of the good Samaritan. A man going down from Jerusalem to Jericho is assaulted, robbed, left for dead. A priest and a Levite see him, but they pass him by. The Samaritan, who should be his enemy, has compassion on him, tends to his wounds, and helps him to safety.

I hear my brothers and sisters of color saying that an injustice has been done to them and they are wounded. You and I may not be the ones who assaulted, robbed, or committed an injustice against them, but if we satisfy ourselves with just not being the robber and walk on by, we're no better than the priest and the Levite. If there's some way that we can have compassion on our brothers and sisters, tend to their wounds, and support them to a place of safety, then we are living as Jesus asks us to live.

And what if we're also a victim? What if we've been beaten and robbed by a sinful, biased culture into thinking our hearts are free of hatred? Maybe we've been left in a hole, blind to our own failings. If so, Saundra and other people of color may help us to a place of spiritual healing and truth.

There's nothing special about me. I'm an everyday Christian doing my best to follow God in challenging times. I'm like the stained-glass windows in my church. In the dark, those windows are useless. You can't see through them. They're unimpressive as artwork. But when light shines through them, they're breathtaking.

Yes, I'm just a middle-aged white woman from Rhode Island living a fairly unremarkable life of faith. But when the light of Christ shines through me, stand back, baby.

So here I am.

Will you join me?

COLORFUL CONVERSATION WITH PATRICIA RAYBON

"Can racial conversations open the door for friendships?" is a great question for a couple of reasons. It implies that conversation draws people together, but it also suggests conversations around the race issue can be more than about race. So I would answer it this way: I am sure that, during my lifetime, especially in the course of giving workshops on race, I have seen people's hearts and minds change. But I am more aware of how conversations about everyday life and where we find commonalities in our challenges—that is, common experiences in our families, our work lives, faith lives, all of those things—are often where people connect the deepest. And then after that connection, we can talk most effectively about race.

When I first started doing diversity awareness training, I would always begin with an icebreaker to help people feel comfortable before we start talking about the hard issue of race. One way I did that was to invite everybody to sing a couple of choruses of "Amazing Grace" with me, because it's a hymn almost everybody knows. Then I would talk about the background and history of the song. The author, John Newton, was a slave trader. In the middle of a storm on the ocean, on a slave ship, Newton asked the Lord to save them all. God changed his heart, and from that came "Amazing Grace." The first stanza includes the phrase, "That saved a wretch like me." All the words of the song describe what happens when it is time to change.

As we sang in those trainings, people often really struggled because they had a very deep connection with the song but were not aware of the slave-trading history. When confronted with this information, I've seen two reactions. The first is fear. But the second is people saying, "Wow, I never knew that, and I need to learn more about it." But we couldn't have that conversation until we sang the song together.

Of course, even after you've connected with someone, don't expect your black friends to be your experts or your teachers. In light of the complexity of the history of this country, it is asking a lot from somebody to mentor their church, Sunday school, or book club through race issues because of the color of their skin. As my husband used to say, "Here are ten books. Read them. Then we can have a conversation." We all, as the church and as a people, need to do some reading and learning.

But then we also need to be able to step back at times and breathe. I grew up under Jim Crow laws and came of age during the Civil Rights era. I was, in fact, born in a segregated hospital. I used to try to talk about these things all the time. But what I've learned is that I am better at it when I take some breaks from the conversation. When it's time to delve into the conversation about race, God shows me who and where I need to engage. It may be a workshop at church, or it may be with a neighbor or a friend.

Here is my point to ponder: this topic is traumatizing in our country. People have been wounded in the deepest ways around race issues. What we can offer each other, especially in the church, is grace. When somebody says, "I am not ready," we can say, "Okay."

When somebody says, "I want to learn more," we can say, "Here are some resources." When somebody says, "Let's go to a play together," maybe the play will stimulate some conversation. But we should not ask any one person to take on all the burden of this work. It is too much. It is too hard. Two are better than one. And three or four are better yet. We have to do this together, in love and in grace, seeking the Holy Spirit's help, because on our own we will fail every time.

PATRICIA RAYBON is an award-winning Colorado author, essayist, and novelist who writes stories of faith and mystery. Her debut 1920s mystery novel, *All That Is Secret*, is a *Parade Magazine* Fall 2021 "Mysteries We Love" selection and a *Masterpiece on PBS* "Best Mystery Books of 2021" selection "As Recommended by Bestselling Authors." Her ethnicity is African American.

STEP 1: COMMIT TO ENGAGE IN THE CONVERSATION.

Maybe you've had thoughts and concerns similar to Saundra's or Lori's when it comes to engaging in hard conversations about race. You may have different reasons for holding back.

Some of us live in fairly homogenous areas, so people who differ from us are not easily available. Others live in places of intense unrest, where a misunderstanding can lead to explosive results in the community. There are as many reasons to hold back as there are readers. Or perhaps you are fully engaged in the work, but you're not seeing other Christians around you participating. You're frustrated and feeling alone. You're looking for language to help others of your skin color see the "on-ramp" for engaging in racial healing. Like Saundra and Lori did, prayerfully consider your why. Write it down so you can refer to it when your confidence waivers.

The first step is to commit to engage in the conversation about race—about where we are and where we need to go, about what we each need to do to get there together. Do that. Commit. And ask God for the courage to take the next step.

Scripture

Reflect on Luke 10:25–37, the parable Jesus told about the good Samaritan and its implications for this conversation. Consider also this verse from the story of Joseph and his brothers in Genesis 42:21, "Then they said to one another, 'In truth we are guilty concerning our brother, in that we saw the distress of his soul, when he begged us and we did not listen. That is why this distress has come upon us.'"

What light do these passages shed on how you should respond to the work of racial healing?

Starting Places

- Share your commitment to engage in a conversation about racial healing with one other believer and ask him or her to hold you accountable.
- If you have no friends from other ethnic backgrounds, talk with your pastor or another mature believer and identify someone in your congregation who may be open to having a conversation with you.
- You may enjoy visiting a church or a Bible study where there are people of other skin colors. Introduce yourself as a Christian wanting to get to know people from different ethnicities and perhaps have conversations about working together toward racial healing.

Chapter Two

ASK BETTER QUESTIONS

NEVER UNDERESTIMATE THE VALUE of asking the right question.

In ancient Jewish culture, the art of asking questions was highly valued. When the rabbis taught, their students interrupted with questions, challenges, and more questions. This wasn't considered rude; it was their way of learning. This is why we find Jesus in the temple at age twelve "sitting among the teachers, listening to them and asking them questions" (Luke 2:46).

Unfortunately, we've all been guilty of beginning argumentative conversations that began with accusatory, leading, or loaded questions. But there are questions that provide keys to opening real conversation.

In the following exchange, we are going to explore the value of the question, "Am I a racist?" We'll also explore questions that prove to be more productive starting places for conversations around ethnicity and conflict over race. We invite you at the end to consider questions that you may use that engage people in collaborative and effective conversation on this topic. No one question will eliminate all conflict, but the right question can create a safer atmosphere for a productive exchange.

WHAT TYPES OF QUESTIONS ENCOURAGE PRODUCTIVE CONVERSATIONS?

Lori

Often we get hung up on the wrong questions. Racism is a complicated issue, so it's easy to understand why. But one of the things we need to realize is that sometimes we're avoiding asking the *right* questions. Because the right questions are hard. I may have it wrong, but here goes.

The question we're often challenged to ask ourselves in the mirror is, "Am I racist?" From news anchors to pastors, activists to entertainers, every talking head of our times summons us to examine our hidden prejudices and call out our inner racist. We're supposed to reflect, to confess, repent, change, progress, evolve.

There's a problem, though. First with the question.

"Am I a racist?" begs a yes or no answer. We like to grade ourselves on a curve; so, since we likely score better on this question than, say, Nazis or the KKK, we give ourselves a passing grade and respond, no. No, I'm not even tempted to don a white hood. Therefore, I'm not a racist.

This is problematic logic. Just because we aren't as hateful or violent as an extremist group doesn't mean we don't have areas needing growth and change. By simply saying we're not racist and moving on, we may be avoiding doing some hard work that could lead to inner personal and interpersonal growth.

Second, even if we've prayerfully wrestled with this question and risen from our knees with the understanding that we aren't essentially racist, someone will likely tell us we just aren't woke enough or aware enough or authoritative enough on the topic to draw that conclusion.

Or they'll tell us we're blind to our own condition. Or we didn't truly understand the question. Or we didn't appreciate the full definition of racism as determined by today's standard.

Of course, that feedback may hold shades of truth, but the ambiguity leaves us likely to become victims of a vague guilt and nagging doubt from the evil one with no effective action steps to address the real issue. We flail about trying to bat this phantom racism away like an annoying gnat, but it keeps buzzing about, distracting us from what may be actual truth.

It's a frustrating exercise to be told that on this particular topic we can't possibly be trusted to come to an informed decision through prayerful discussion with God. This fruitless cycle leaves Christians who are sincerely trying not to be racist frustrated and in despair, while those who do harbor hatred of others based on skin color are probably not losing sleep. (I hesitate to call these people Christians, though they may use that term for themselves, because hating is antithetical to following Jesus.)

Third, the notion that there are different "races" is problematic for most Bible believers who understand that there is one human race, designed thoughtfully and creatively by God, with a variety of skin colors, cultures, and ethnicities. "Am I racist?" they may ask. "I believe there's only one race, and since God is for it, so am I," they answer. But how does that help us on a practical level?

Of course I don't consider myself racist. I've grown up believing people are created equal and that all humans deserve respect, dignity, and love. I accept the idea that I have blind spots and am open to correction, but I am open. Ergo, I respond, no, I'm not racist. Still, after hearing the cries of my brothers and sisters of color, I'm not comfortable just leaving it at that. And so I conclude that maybe I've started with the wrong question.

Then there's the second problem. Most of us begin reflecting on our own contribution to the problem of racial tension in our times by looking in the wrong mirror. If we rely on current cultural standards to tell us whether or not we're racist, that's a precarious perch. Words and terms change. New societal measures evolve. Every generation develops its own code, and that can leave the generations before floundering due to misinformation, not true prejudice. So society isn't a great mirror.

Some of us look to people of other ethnicities or skin colors to answer the question for us. "I'm your friend. Tell me, do you think I'm racist? Am I enough of what you need to qualify as 'not part of the problem'?" Again, it's an understandable mirror to ask those who feel oppressed if they see us as part of their oppression, but who can say what contributes to their answers? Is racism a problem only for people of one skin color? Could racism inhabit people with darker skin? And if we clear the bar for our friend's racism test, does that mean we'll be accepted by every person of every color and ethnicity? How does that work? Do they issue us some kind of card? Perhaps other people are also an imperfect mirror.

So if self-reflection, societal feedback, and peer approval are not necessarily accurate mirrors on the question of racism, what is? I believe, and I'm guessing you agree, that the Bible is the only reliable mirror and that God's teaching is clear on what behaviors, thoughts, and actions are representative of someone full of love and free from prejudice.

When I go to God's Word, as is my practice for all of life's major quandaries, I find myself thinking there are more productive questions leading to ethnic unity than to simply ask, "Am I a racist?" These questions address the core issue but approach it from angles that are more likely to lead to widespread corrective action. These questions can bring us to places of repentance, of desiring continued growth, and to do kingdom work, and they're the questions we're exploring in this book.

Do I love the way Jesus loves? Do I love everyone Jesus considers to be my neighbor? Are there ways I could love people better or communicate my love clearer?

How can I show love to those who are expressing anger, pain, and desperation at a system they've experienced as unfair?

Am I engaging with people in my community who look different from me? Why or why not?

Do the demographics of my church reflect the demographics of my community? Of the world? Why or why not? Is there room for improvement? What would improvement look like?

Am I willing to be uncomfortable in order to help people who don't feel included or accepted in God's family feel more at home? What does that look like? What's biblically non-negotiable and what's simply a matter of culture or tradition that can be modified?

Am I quick to listen, slow to speak, and slow to anger?

Do I care enough about Christians of color to forget about myself and listen to them talk about their experiences and their parents' experiences without judgment or defensiveness?

God loves justice. Are there actions I can take that would further the cause of justice in my community?

If I'm a Christian of color, am I willing to see beyond the skin of my Caucasian brothers and sisters and see them the way I want to be seen, as individuals worthy of respect and acceptance? How do I communicate this?

God loves justice. Are there actions I can take that would further the cause of justice in my community? Or have I given up on justice this side of glory? Have I stopped trying because it's hard or because I'm not directly impacted? Have I lost hope, and if so, can I repent of my own hopelessness and return to the work in faith?

Am I living in obedience to God's full call on my life? Are there ways I've placed my own comfort first over delivering the good news of Jesus or of engaging in the ministry of reconciliation to people who are from different cultures or ethnicities?

Am I growing spiritually, in ever-increasing measure, in faith, virtue, knowledge, self-control, steadfastness, godliness, brotherly affection, and love so that I am effective and fruitful in my faith?

Would others say my life is marked by truth and love, both spoken and lived? Is the legacy I leave likely to be one of reconciliation, sacrificial living, and bringing glory to Jesus's name? What does the next generation around me observe in my unguarded moments? Does what I do back up what I say should be done?

Can we imagine for a moment that if we worked with some of these questions, we might make a dent in reducing racism, deepening Christian community, and spreading the gospel at the same time?

It's antithetical to living for Christ to harbor racism, but "Am I a racist?" is, too often, a dead-end question that doesn't lead to helpful answers. The Bible, however, is replete with worthy questions and challenges that lead any heart that is filled with the Holy Spirit to Christ-centered growth and change.

If the question you're asking yourself in this time in our generation leads you to change nothing, then you're asking the wrong question. And if you're not asking any questions, then, loved one, maybe you're not even paying attention.

People are taking to the streets crying out for change. All change is not equal. Some just leads us into variations of our old discriminations. Let's begin asking the questions our God asks in order to increase the likelihood that we will move forward together toward him and not just twist in an equally damaging direction.

Saundra

To ask "Am I a racist?" is indeed a question with many flaws. It is a rare person who would respond in the affirmative. As with many speculative questions, our initial response is to distance ourselves as much as possible from being labeled negatively.

When Lori first brought this question into our conversation, I immediately thought, *Of course I'm not a racist; I'm of the minority group.* This initial response alone reflects part of the problem and why it is important to ask the right questions.

In researching what it means to be a racist, most of us associate it with those who intentionally discriminate based on the color of a person's skin. If you are not someone who would physically harm, economically limit, or otherwise block opportunities in a person's life, you get to mark the "no" box beside racist.

Like Lori, I associated the term with *extremist.* Those, I label based on their history of prejudice against specific groups of people. Since I have not personally participated in any such events or affiliated with any groups involved in this type of extreme behavior, I excluded myself from any association with this label. Plus, as a person from a historically oppressed group, calling myself a racist sounded like an oxymoron. Can one be both the oppressed and the oppressor?

As I evaluated my feelings on this topic, I noticed my responses and attitude toward certain groups of people were not focused on their skin color but on the culture with which they associate. I've judged certain groups of people to be more prone to apathy and others more intellectually adept simply based on their ethnicity. I am not a racist in my eyes, but I do see instances in my life where I am culturally insensitive.

Cultural insensitivity can take many forms, from offensive words to stereotypes resulting in false beliefs about groups of people within a particular culture to a lack of respect for different cultural values. Our lack of understanding about other cultures creates a gap into which we can fall. A gap worsened by our need for better parameters around communicating with different cultures.

During a recently heated time in the media, an Asian American friend posted a video on social media that brought to light my own need for greater cultural sensitivity. She stated, "I feel angry and sad and vulnerable and helpless trying to put my mind around the rising anti-Asian hate crimes that have been taking place." She shared that she avoided grocery stores during the 2020 pandemic lockdown, not because of her fear of getting the virus, but because of her fear of being yelled at or harmed because of her Asian DNA.

I had heard people refer to the coronavirus as the China virus or the Asian flu. I had not considered how these descriptors could translate into permission to discriminate. Those who made these comments were not trying to hurt my Asian friend. Some said it in humor, trying to lighten the blow of a difficult season. Some said it as a way to identify the geographic locale of the first outbreak. Regardless of the motive behind the words, the cultural insensitivity remains, and a group of people aches.

My friend described a current Western view of strength as being like an oak tree that stands firm under stress and how, in the Asian culture, strength is often viewed as being like bamboo with the ability to bend and bend without breaking. Neither viewpoint is better than the other, as both standing and bending are part of living, but they provide a great example of how our cultural vantage point can affect how we may respond to different situations. I don't want to be a part of the bending process in the life of others who don't look like me.

> *Christians who are effective at racial reconciliation can navigate cultural boundaries with sensitivity and communicate from the place of a heart yielded to loving well.*

Racism is not a color issue; it's a cultural insensitivity issue. It is what happens when there is a lack of respect and appreciation for diversity. Culture is part of God's many gifts to us. It provides a richness to our experiences that can only be enjoyed when we become aware of the different colors, flavors, textures, and patterns in life. Recognizing a person's particular culture affirms their contributions to humanity and imparts a sense of belonging.

Christians who are effective at racial reconciliation can navigate cultural boundaries with sensitivity and communicate from the place of a heart yielded to loving well. In the article "Issues for the Church in a Multi-Racial Society," John Root states, "Racism is not simply a garment that people willingly put on, it is also an aroma that we unwittingly acquire. Simply to condemn extreme groups is ineffective; sin (as ever) is more subtle, complex and deep rooted than that."[1]

The questions I'm asking myself on this journey are directed at identifying the places where thoughts and beliefs have taken root and affect how I interact with those of different cultures—excavating the areas of my heart needing to be removed to allow more room for the Holy Spirit.

The spiritual posture I ask you to enter this time of excavation with is one reflective of David's in Psalm 139:23–24, "Search me, God, and know my heart; Put me to the test and know my anxious thoughts; And see if there is any hurtful way in me, And lead me in the everlasting way" (NASB).

When you begin a housing project, the contractor starts with excavation. The steps needed to build an earthly dwelling suitable for someone to live in are similar to preparing a dwelling place for God within our hearts.

The first stage is to identify the demarcation lines around the area to be addressed. This process, known as *rough staking*, involves placing stakes in the ground to make it easy to see what is inside and what is outside the boundary lines. These markers ensure we stay within safe parameters. As Lori and I go deeper into conversation, the stakes placed are the boundary lines of the Word of God.

Once you've identified what's inside the lines, you can see what needs to be removed to clear the space. Any beliefs or concepts that do not align with the desired outcome are cut away. Vegetation is pulled, roots and all. This process is messy and can look disruptive on the surface. What was once smooth becomes chaotic. Also, decisions must be made about what to do with the debris you've unearthed.

This *clearing stage* is where guilt, shame, fear, anger, hurt, trauma, and other emotions around cultural pain will be exposed. Once brought to the surface, you will need a place to leave this debris. I recommend taking them to the cross. As you process through the clearing stage's bumpy terrain, don't get overcome by what you find under the surface. Don't allow it to be a stumbling block to moving to the next phase.

*External growth before inner growth
is a setup for a fall.*

The next stage of excavation is the *testing phase*. Here is where the soil is evaluated to determine its structural integrity. You don't want to build on soil unable to withstand the pressure of growth and expansion. As God has allowed my readership and impact to grow, I've encountered more character tests. Temptations arise out of nowhere, and the soil of my heart is called into question. External growth before inner growth is a setup for a fall. But anything built on ground that has endured the process of testing can remain standing when challenged.

The testing of a heart ready to love well involves people. The test of communicating with someone who doesn't share your beliefs. The test of extending grace when someone is not being gracious. The test of offering mercy to someone who does not deserve it. The test of restraint when the wounded lash out in pain. The test of forgiveness when there have been no signs of remorse. You need not worry about looking for the tests. They will come to you. Instead, focus on what you learn from each test and use the data to grow.

The final stage is the *design execution phase*. Now, what has been envisioned on paper is birthed into reality. Theory and doctrine become a living testimony of walking it out in real time. The details begin to come together to erect something that looks like the home you desired to build. This is the stage right before inhabitation.

This stage requires an understanding of the design. It's hard to execute something you can't envision. The Bible shares a beautiful vision of God's design in Revelation 7:9: "After this I looked, and there before me was a great multitude that no one could count, from every nation, tribe, people and language, standing before the throne and before the Lamb" (NIV). Let this be what we work toward building on earth as in heaven.

COLORFUL CONVERSATION WITH JO SAXTON

I don't think we can move forward without the ability to express how we feel. I am reminded of the ongoing work in South Africa. Archbishop Desmond Tutu in his book *No Future Without Forgiveness* talks about the need for reconciliation and how you cannot have it without truth. He says that sometimes when people have this idea of reconciliation, they think it's going to get better. Actually, it gets worse because you cannot move forward until you name and acknowledge what's going on. As long as we treat racism as the taboo that we dare not speak of, we will not heal. We cannot heal it by politeness. I think we have put politeness above equity. People want you to not show any emotion or articulate any pain. It is a very high price for somebody to pay. I should say, it also doesn't work.

There comes a point for us in leadership where we have to say, "Ignoring the pain isn't the right thing to do." We must choose to be a leader—someone who is intentional with their influence, rather than someone who is popular but generally moved by opinions more than truth. True leaders ask, "What direction are we meant to go in?" They understand that not everybody is going to like or follow their path, and that's okay.

If we are going to lead through conversations about race and in the midst of difficult circumstances, we have to say, "Are we doing the right thing before God?" Because living out your calling is never about the pleasures of the people around you; it's a response to God.

A number of years ago, I was involved in a church plant and some-body on my team mentioned their concern about me, referencing a particular social justice movement. They said to me, "It makes people feel uncomfortable, so they are not funding you. If you don't say it, you'll be able to secure more resources." This was meant to be kind; it really was. But as a leader, this kind of comment places you in this really vulnerable position, because it is not just your job at stake. Your decisions now affect other people's jobs and economic opportunities.

Some people operate in conversations as a leader without real-izing they don't have authority on that specific topic. You may have authority in preaching or administration, but do not have any Black, Asian, Latino, indigenous, or immigrant friends. When your under-standing of your leadership context does not include the insights and lived experiences of other groups of people, your picture is incomplete.

Sometimes leaders lead by trying to explain somebody else's experience, and they end up saying things like, "You know, what that person meant was . . ." Their intent may be to keep the peace, but inadvertently they minimize the experience of the most vulnerable people who have been marginalized. It becomes a kind of cheap, cover-up version of reconciliation.

Or instead of leading, they actually stop a conversation too soon— you don't get through the pain barrier. Because now it's about managing people by saying, "Okay, I know you don't want to be called racist." When in fact no one is actually calling anyone a racist; they are just asking a question about the intentions of a person's questionable comments. This hiding from confrontation has become the reality of the conversation about racism (or, really, many difficult topics). Everything becomes obscured by the emotion of the moment. Some go on the offense by trying to take charge, and others are defensive, saying, "Don't say that. Don't say the R-word to me." I find those moments difficult because avoiding the deeper, more honest conversation is costly for the BIPOC person (Black, Indigenous, and People of Color) involved. It's costly to have to manage someone who is on the offensive, attempting to subordinate your experiences. It's also costly to manage the defensive person who has moved the conversation to focus on their own feelings. This forces the question, "Is it worth it?"

Is it worth the potential pain and frustration to have a conversation?

If you're not going to be heard, if your experiences are going to be minimized or overlooked, or if it's about the other person getting defensive, then no, it isn't.

But if the conversation is going to be real and honest, if there is a willingness to listen and an openness for a genuine deeper conversation, then yes. It's still costly, but it could be worth it.

JO SAXTON is a leadership coach, author, speaker, and co-host of *Lead Stories Podcast*. Her ethnicity is Nigerian and British.

STEP 2: ASK BETTER QUESTIONS—LOOK IN THE RIGHT MIRROR.

What have you learned from wrestling with the question "Am I racist?" Do you find it useful to ask of yourself or others? How can the other questions listed in this chapter help lead in the direction of racial reconciliation?

What other questions do you believe are useful? What are the risks of asking society or other people to answer the question for us? What benefit is there of relying on the Bible to be our mirror on this journey toward ridding ourselves of prejudice?

Perhaps your family does have an ancestral history of racism or prejudice. How do you approach the questions in this chapter? What do you do, no matter what color your skin, when you realize you are being culturally insensitive, prejudicial of a certain ethnicity, or judgmental based on skin color or country of origin? What does God's Word command you to do?

Scripture

Proverbs 18:1–2 says this: "Whoever isolates himself seeks his own desire; he breaks out against all sound judgment. A fool takes no pleasure in understanding, but only in expressing his opinion."

How can it be helpful in having a conversation about race to begin with making sure we're asking questions and asking the right questions?

What is the danger of remaining alone in our own mirrors when considering whether we are racist?

Have you ever looked into a fun house mirror or tried to get an accurate view of yourself from a broken mirror? What is the importance of all of us—people of every color—using the same mirror when considering these questions? What is the danger of using the wrong one?

Consider what James has to say about this in James 1:23–25. How can we apply this passage to this conversation?

Starting Places

- Commit to step two by opening your Bible. Ask God to lead you in this process and guide you to both the questions and the answers through his Word.

- Ask your pastor or a mature Christian friend what the Bible has to say about how we should treat people of other skin colors and/ or ethnicities.
- Look at the resources listed in the back of this book and choose one book to read. Look for books, movies, or documentaries on aspects of racism and watch one.
- Ask three trusted friends (try to find at least one friend whose skin color is different from yours) if there are areas in which they feel you could grow in loving people of different ethnicities.

Chapter Three

BE QUICK TO LISTEN

We all have a desire to be heard.

The psalmist writes in Psalm 116:1–2, "I love the Lord, because he has heard my voice and my pleas for mercy. Because he inclined his ear to me, therefore I will call on him as long as I live." We have a God who hears.

One vital ministry we have with one another is to listen. One way we grow in our understanding of people whose lives are different from ours is to hear their stories. This can be challenging, painful, and time-consuming, but it is almost always productive in deepening relationships.

For us, we didn't know one another well when we began this project, so one of our initial steps was to simply tell each other our stories. Specifically, we each share, in this chapter and the next, what it's like to be black or white Christians in our times.

We can't fix everything for one another, but we can hear one another out in love. James 1:19 exhorts all believers in this way: "Know this, my beloved brothers: let every person be quick to hear, slow to speak, slow to anger." That's very direct and clear, and we chose to practice that when dialoguing in this book.

As you read chapters 3 and 4, you may sometimes feel as if you're eavesdropping on a very personal exchange. That is by design. We wanted to demonstrate listening to one another and being slow to take offense by allowing each other space to just provide snapshots of our experiences. As you read, consider what you might share with someone else if they asked for your story about being a Christian— with your skin color in our times.

HOW DOES LISTENING ENHANCE THE EFFECTIVENESS OF CONVERSATIONS?

Saundra

My family's car turned down the long driveway. Weeping willow trees flowed on either side, ushering us in. My friend Linda was at the car door before my six-year-old mind could take in my surroundings. It was my first playdate at a white friend's home.

Linda's family owned an estate with horses and a pool. I had experience with neither. Yet the vast differences in our socioeconomic status were not a barrier to the friendship that blossomed during our first year in school. When all the other kids would run out for recess to play kickball or chase, you could find the two of us begging the teacher to let us spend the time coloring or reading. In Linda, I had found someone who embraced her nerdy tendencies just as much as I had mine. That bond grew into a friendship we were happy to extend beyond the school day.

The hot Georgia humidity caused us to move our play day from the expansive outdoor grounds of Linda's home to the inside of what I now know was a colonial-style house.

It was a beautiful day of friendship and shared experiences—until the moment it wasn't. At dinner time, Linda's mom called us to the table. Overflowing platters of chicken, rolls, and vegetables were set before us. Before the first spoonful of green beans found their place on my plate, Linda leaned over to whisper, "That's my MeMe. She's black."

MeMe busied herself with making sure everyone had what they

needed before returning to the kitchen. She didn't join us for the meal and was not seen again until it was time for the plates to be cleared and dessert served. MeMe was an important but invisible part of Linda's household. Despite her role as the one who provided delicious meals for the family, cared for Linda, and supplied ongoing household support, the only description Linda offered to me was in reference to her race.

From that early experience, I began to develop the belief that no matter how good I was at something, my blackness would always be the first thing people see. The problem was not with the color of my skin but with the cultural biases of the times. Unfortunately, my six-year-old mind could not differentiate the two. Long after the playdate ended, I saw my race as a handicap to overcome.

Studies show we begin to form a first impression of a person within the first seven seconds of the encounter.[1] From that momentary contact, we decide if we believe someone is trustworthy, competent, or reliable. There are countless tips for how to improve your first impression, but they fail to share how to improve that impression if it is based on the color of your skin. Even if I make good eye contact, smile, project a friendly voice tone, or any other tactics, I still cannot change others' observational bias projected upon me based solely on my race.

We don't talk about how experiencing bias and prejudice as a child affects the adult you will one day become. We understand that children who are bullied can grow up feeling insecure or "less than." We appreciate the difficulty of navigating the social politics of high school when youth don't fit in with the cool kids. But what about the psychology of living in a culture where your race is not viewed as equal? It changes you from the inside out.

When you grow up as the target of prejudice, it can have lasting adverse effects. Child development specialists report it is not uncommon for such children to feel hopeless and enraged, and to experience depressed, anxious, and angry moods which they may be hard-pressed to articulate or manage.[2] For others, it can result in a drive to succeed—sometimes an unhealthy motivation to excel at all costs.

As a workaholic with perfectionist tendencies, overcoming biases became a personal goal. It pushed me to pursue opportunities where I did not see many faces that looked like my own. While my friends were enjoying the summer of our sixteenth birthdays, I was working five hours a day in a university lab. When given the option to take standard high school classes that I could easily pass with an A or push myself by taking honors classes, I chose the one with the least diverse representation. I regularly placed myself in uncomfortable situations where I was "the lonely only." The only black face in a sea of white. If I couldn't change someone's first impression, I would make sure their final opinion would have more substance by which to judge.

It meant pushing myself to always exceed expectations. Some may praise this mindset as being an outstanding work ethic. I saw it as the plight of being black. Either you became great, or you remained hidden behind the screen of your brown skin. The internal drive had little to do with personality and everything to do with learned behavior based on past prejudice.

College and medical school were a continuation of the same mindset. If I got enough degrees, I would not have to deal with unconscious bias. Somewhere in my youthful thinking, I believed that I could conceal my race behind the white coat of my profession.

I finished my college and medical school training at the age of twenty-six, with a full expectation of no longer having to feel bound by systemic racism. I had the MD degree I had been striving for, but little did I know how ineffective it would be in giving me any protection against prejudice. It actually became the gate God used to address this issue of the heart in not only my life but also in that of an unsuspecting family.

It was Iron Bowl Saturday evening, and there wasn't an empty seat in the emergency room. If you are not from Alabama, let me explain this phenomenon to you. Every year, Auburn and Alabama play each other. Neighbors become enemies. Some pastors won't even mention the two teams because it will cause an uproar among their body of believers. I'm a University of Georgia graduate, so I don't have a dog in that fight. But for those in the city where I practice medicine, the Iron Bowl is a big deal. They are serious about their football.

Sometimes they take it a little too seriously. Hours cheering for their favorite college football team or yelling when a ball is dropped or a field goal missed can raise the blood pressure to dangerous levels. On this particular Saturday, the game was one that had everyone on the edge of their seats, resulting in an ER full of people with chest pain and shortness of breath. It also happened to be my first time working within this hospital system, and my introduction to life as a black female physician working in the South.

With the patient's chart in hand, I stepped into Exam Room #12. I had barely finished introducing myself before the patient abruptly stated, "I've never had a colored doctor."

There was a pregnant silence in the room. Everyone waited to see what would be birthed out of the moment. I could hear my heartbeat without the need for a stethoscope. The air in the room felt insufficient. A range of emotions hit me all at once: hurt, embarrassment, anger, fear, and anxiety. The thing I had tried to outrun was a present reality I had to address.

The patient sat on the exam table, having stated what for him was a simple matter of truth. He had never had a physician who was not white. His tone was not malicious. He didn't have hate in his eyes. He actually smiled one of the sweetest smiles as he plunged this verbal dagger into me.

Surrounding the bedside were his wife and his daughter, staring with their mouths agape, unsure of what to say next. The inappropriateness of his comment was further highlighted by the flush of red coloring both of their cheeks.

Noticing the horrified look on the faces of his family, he quickly followed with, "I'm not against it. I just have never had one."

I look back at this moment and marvel at the workings of the Holy Spirit. There are times to fight back with your words, but there are also times to give a gentle reply. In a matter of seconds, I was able to discern that it was not fair for me to assume this man was a racist based solely on his first comment. Like me, he had possibly been in situations where he had witnessed prejudice, injustice, and discrimination toward others by adult mentors. It would not be fair for me to judge him before taking the time to get to know him beyond my first impression.

"Lucky you! I will be your first," I retorted, breaking through the tension with a little humor.

Despite our rough and unusual beginning, this patient and his family became adamant supporters of my work. They told everyone in the community about the new doctor they met in the hospital. Their friends started signing up for appointments; most of them also had never had a black or a female doctor. Now, reflecting on over twenty years of caring for this community and looking back on the growth that's happened, it all began with one man willing to start a hard conversation.

I didn't realize how far we had come in building that doctor-patient relationship until years later when this same gentleman found himself back in the hospital. On this evening, one of my colleagues was covering for me in the ER. You can imagine my surprise when I received a text stating, "Saundra, I have one of your patients here who is refusing my care. He only wants your recommendation." Oh, the irony of my white male colleague calling me about my white male patient refusing his care because of the trust he had developed for his black female physician!

As I grabbed my white coat and headed to my car, I couldn't help but reflect on changes in our relationship through the years. The growth we both had to make to get to a place of mutual respect and shared commonalities. Despite our fifty-plus years' difference in age, despite how we were both raised within our respective families, and despite the apparent prejudices we had witnessed modeled by adult figures in our lives, we were able to get to a place of loving and caring for each other like family.

God used this gentleman to show me what it looks like to love my neighbor well, by choosing to listen first rather than react. It meant being patient when he didn't always know the politically correct way to share his feelings. It meant choosing gentleness over aggression. It meant celebrating new grandbabies and taking a moment in the middle of my busy workday to let a proud Pop Pop show me pictures of chubby cheeks and toothless grins. At times it meant laying down my offense and picking up kindness. And other times it meant standing my ground and sharing my hurt with grace and truth. Through it all, we found a place where we could stand together and listen well.

Maybe, like me, you've found the most difficult part is to remain proactive and not reactive when discussing racial issues. When a wound is still tender, it doesn't enjoy being poked. Every media blast about racism, discrimination, or injustice pushes in on the tender places. It takes me back to the dinner table in Linda's home where I felt marginalized, the classrooms where I felt alone, and the ER where I felt unappreciated. It is a reminder that time alone does not heal, it just conceals until the next opportunity arises for it to resurface. So when we feel the pain of that wound being poked, do we poke back, or do we look for ways to heal?

Let's choose healing. Now the real work begins in seeing what that looks like to be quick to listen and asking how we can proactively be a part of the healing process.

Lori

I don't know about you, but Saundra's description of her playdate with Linda delivered a punch that left me breathless, imagining a six-year-old trying to process her little friend's introduction of MeMe, distinguishing her solely by skin color. It's too easy to explain it away as a child's interpretation of roles, her immature description of this important woman in the family's life. It's very likely that she was reflecting what the adults around her said about MeMe. So often we think we're only teaching children when we speak directly to them about a topic and don't factor in the myriad indirect messages we're sending or that they're receiving during all their waking hours.

Children and teens often hang on the periphery of our private conversations, learning more from our example than from our sporadic instruction. The collective tutorial of our unguarded speech, the radio stations we tune in to hear, the news channels we watch, and the groupthink of our friends and extended family all contribute to their understanding of culture. Reading one book with them on equality or having a couple of directed conversations about how we treat everyone equally, won't undo the cumulative saturation of countless overheard hours. Maybe the first listening we need to do is to hear how our own words may sound to others.

The situation was more poignant because Linda was Saundra's friend. Saundra was wide-open emotionally and happy to be in a relationship where she felt welcome for being herself. It's as if as she was settling into that friendship until a sudden tilt in perceived power left her scrambling for balance and stability.

I don't know if Saundra talked about the situation with her parents or another trusted adult, but I'm guessing not. Shame is a silencer. Even children with rich, trusting relationships with their parents will hesitate to share situations that caused them to feel shame. And how confusing is that moment for a child. Here was a friend who was different from the other children the same way Saundra was, and yet here, Saundra was pricked by a thorn on this rosy relationship. Hurt in a way that impacted her for years.

Our culture tends to romanticize children, and they do, of course, have a certain innocence in approaching the world. Still, anyone who spends time with children will testify that they can also exhibit selfishness, self-centeredness, and unkindness. Sin shows itself early, and we must be diligent to teach our children well.

My children attended weekly Bible club, in which they were the minority. I remember my daughter's first visit when she was just a preschooler. I hadn't factored in my artistic child's penchant for being detailed about color. When she came home, I asked if she enjoyed her time.

"Yes," she said excitedly with a nod, "I sat next to a tea-colored boy, and across from me was a honey-colored girl."

She went on with other descriptors as I held my breath, praying that each would be a flattering adjective (they were.) I understood why this was her initial fascination but wondered how to expand her vision beyond skin color. First, I asked her to describe her own skin color.

"Maybe brown-ishy cream."

When I explained that most people would call her white, she was annoyed. "Well, I'm definitely not white. That's silly! People are wrong."

On the way to Bible club the next week, I suggested she make it a goal to learn children's names. The next week, I asked her to remember what three children said about the Bible story.

This weekly relationship-building scavenger hunt may have happened naturally, but I wanted to help her learn how to get to know people and get past surface understandings. I'm continually amazed at how willing adults are to live on the surface of relationships and not dive deeper.

I do believe that left to our own, without the help of the Holy Spirit, people can become victims of first impressions, children can grow up believing they are *lesser than* based on others' reactions to them, and we can propagate a culture of prejudice and mistrust. Within the church, however, I see hope.

One of my friends grew up in the Philippines, and she talks about growing up with neighbors who believed beauty could be measured by the lightness of one's skin. As the darkest-skinned sister of three girls, she recalls these neighbors rating their beauty as they passed, with her sisters always faring better than she.

"That affected me as a young teen, but then I emerged from that. I see the beauty of my design because I know Jesus." Her initial perspective was clearly impacted by those around her, but Jesus had the last word on her understanding of herself and her beauty. I admire that, while still wishing she hadn't been subjected to a melanin-based standard of beauty.

The message I received as a child was that I was born guilty by virtue of my skin color. I was taught that I could make a difference by being different from my ancestors, but by my teens, that didn't feel as though it were true. No matter how loving I was, it seemed that I wasn't enough to make a difference, because other white people weren't loving. My contribution seemed so small, it was worthless, as if nothing would erase the guilt of a color I didn't choose.

Here, too, is where I've found freedom in Christ, because he designed me and accepts me completely just as I am. My understanding from Scripture is that I am not held individually responsible for the sins of other generations (Jeremiah 31:29–30), but I am still impacted by the consequence of their sins, as my children will be if I don't make godly choices (Jeremiah 32:18). My redemption comes from Jesus, not from any other human, and I live in that freedom which gives me the security to listen with an open heart to those who are angry with, or mistrusting of, anyone who looks like me.

> *In Christ, we can celebrate our design and revel in his design of others.*

Saundra strove to be excellent enough to "overcome" her blackness, and I strove to be loving enough to "overcome" my whiteness, but both of us found our striving insufficient because we were striving toward a lesser story than the one to which we've been called. In Christ alone are we overcomers. In Christ, we can celebrate our design and revel in his design of others. Saundra and I didn't find one another because she's an excellent doctor or because I've worked to be different from past generations of white people. We found one another because we both write for Jesus, and it's because of Christ that we found the courage to begin this conversation.

But I admit that the conversation has already been painfully eye-opening. When Saundra described her experience with the man who'd never had a doctor like her before, I was saddened that she felt that rush of "hurt, embarrassment, anger, fear, and anxiety." After all the sacrifice and hard work that it took to become a doctor, a doctor is all people should see. The man's comment was so disheartening!

But I could also identify with the wife and daughter holding their breath at their husband's/father's words. My dad was a man of his generation, but no one ever described him as prejudiced or racist. He was a fire chief, and within the fire department, his only measure of a person was if they were committed to being excellent at serving their community. Still, he became an adult in the 1950s, and the culture has shifted significantly since the times when his first thoughts about culture were formed. That led to some learning moments.

I remember the first time he had a male nurse. He remarked about it aloud, and the nurse responded similarly to the way Saundra responded to her patient. The nurse listened to my dad and heard him in the context of his generation. His correction was gentle and kind. Thank God for people who are changing the world, not just by breaking professional barriers but also by being people of mercy and grace when they do.

My dad had a tender heart, but whatever came into his mind emerged from his mouth, and it wasn't always politically correct. Sometimes his words were an indication of a prejudice he had to work through (especially when it came to accepting female firefighters— something he came to embrace before many others did). But most often, it was simply an indication that he hadn't kept up with evolving language. It came to be a practice for him to check in with me or one of my teens about words or terms he planned to use before delivering a presentation, a training, or giving a speech. To me, that was a sign that he was listening—to me, to younger firefighters, and to the voices of a culture trying to use respectful words reflective for all people.

As uncomfortable as it was sometimes that Dad would just speak what was on his mind, it was also reassuring that you always knew what he was thinking. I suspect many people hide behind silence. Some likely had a negative reaction to being treated by Saundra but would not let a word of it emerge from their mouths in her presence. They would have remained polite but then never returned. This racism cloaked in silence and smiles is why I can believe it's hard for some people of color to trust. It's also why I believe it's better to fumble our way through awkward discussions than to gracefully navigate by muting our inconvenient thoughts. It's harder to hear what people are "saying" with their silence, and misunderstandings arise from guessing.

This isn't easy. I didn't want to teach my daughter not to notice color, because color is part of our design. But I did want to help her find ways to see more than color when getting to know new people. I wouldn't want people to judge my dad based on a statement that honestly reflects his experience. On the other hand, he readily accepted the responsibility of checking his wording with others, once he realized there were changes that he could make to better demonstrate his respect of others. That realization happened because people spoke up and he chose to listen.

We need to arrive at a place ... where we understand the battle against racism to be a shared effort, because we all lose if we don't move forward.

I'm so glad Saundra persevered through every barrier to become the doctor and writer she is. We would be lesser not to have her teaching. In how many other ways have we all been robbed of important voices and contributions that were blocked because of ethnic division and discrimination based on skin color?

We need to arrive at a place (and I believe many of us are there) where we understand the battle against racism to be a shared effort, because we all lose if we don't move forward. We also have to be real about the wounds and scars we'll incur along the way (that's what happens in battles) but commit to moving forward anyway, acknowledging the pain but refusing to let it hold us back from reaching the fullness of expression God desires for all his people. I don't believe God wants Saundra to be wounded for the color of her skin nor me to be paralyzed with guilt for the color of mine.

When we align in Christ, we're better able to recognize that the real enemimes are the evil forces that would pit us against one another and those who embrace those forces rather than resist them. By refusing to hide from one another, even when we may expose our weaknesses and sins, we find a Christ-centered strength from which to work together to achieve a community that embraces equality in transformative and life-affirming ways.

COLORFUL CONVERSATION WITH RACHEL KANG

I've not always had the courage to partake in conversations about race. I've tiptoed around the topic because, as a mixed-race woman, I felt I was never able to pick a side. It wasn't until the summer of 2020 that I fully stepped into my identity and realized I have a great advantage. I have the ability to see from various angles—I have the opportunity to speak into racial tensions and things left unresolved.

I remember, as a young girl, asking my grandmother for a Claddagh ring, a traditional ring that represents part of my Irish heritage. I asked for it because it was something tangible I could cling to that symbolized a part of my family. Growing up, my Native American heritage always resonated deeply within me because my family and I always went to the powwows together. In this, I had physical and tangible experiences that I could carry to remind me of my culture. My husband is Korean, and we try to do the same with our kids. Whether it's books or exposing them to Korean food or cartoon characters, these are tangible things that can help remind my kids who they are.

I see a lot of listening and learning taking place these days. It's necessary to listen to voices that may rub us the wrong way. It's very easy to unfollow someone if they say something we don't like. But sometimes discomfort can be a helpful tool. It can help us realize if there is a discussion that we're not comfortable with or haven't thought about yet.

The work we're doing is nothing new, but it is needed. We have a lot of great leaders who have been initiating conversations about race for decades and have led efforts to bring truth and light by way of sharing intellectual, logical, and brutal facts.

True stories, whether you agree with the conclusions or not, will give you new perspectives and might just change your mind or solidify your previous conclusion. This is why we cannot discount the fact that many are reading books and listening to podcasts in order to learn from diverse voices. Many *are* seeking out the answers for unity and love. The work is hard, slow, and often unseen, but where there is learning there are also walls falling down.

RACHEL MARIE KANG is a New York native, born and raised just outside of New York City. A woman of mixed African American, Native American, Irish, and Dutch descent, she is a graduate of Nyack College with a degree in English with Creative Writing. Her writing has been featured in *Christianity Today*, *Charlotte Magazine*, and *(in)courage*, and she is the author of *Let There Be Art*. Rachel lives and writes from North Carolina at rachelmariekang.com and Instagram at @rachelmariekang.

STEP 3: BE QUICK TO LISTEN.

Before we seek to be understood, it's wise and loving to seek to understand.

We serve a God who hears, a God who listens to our prayers. When we listen to one another, we reflect an aspect of God. One of the simplest ways we can serve one another in this hard conversation about race is to be willing to set our stories aside for a moment and immerse ourselves in our brother's or sister's experience.

Before we seek to be understood, it's wise and loving to seek to understand. To show compassion through patient listening, honest questions, and statements that help our listeners know we've heard them, allowing them to clarify what we've heard incorrectly.

Our society sometimes wrongly communicates that by listening to one another, we will inevitably "slide a slippery slope" into compromising truth. We know this isn't true because of Jesus. He listened to sinners of every type and communicated love while also teaching hard truth. The more we are like him, the more we will listen without fear, seeing it as an act of love, not penance nor the path to compromise.

Commit to step 3, being quick to listen.

Scripture

Listening isn't just a good suggestion but a command of God for all his people written in James 1:19: "Know this, my beloved brothers: let every person be quick to hear, slow to speak." Likewise, Proverbs exhorts God followers with these words in Proverbs 1:5 "Let the wise hear and increase in learning, and the one who understands obtain guidance." Read the story of young Jesus in the temple as recorded in Luke 2:41–52.

What does it say Jesus was doing in Luke 2:46? What are the benefits of the "ministry of listening"?

Starting Places

- Schedule time to sit with a person you know who comes from a different background or whose skin is a color different from yours. Open the conversation by saying, "I'd like to understand more about what it's like to live in our times from your perspective. Would you be willing to tell me your story?" Then listen, in love, and when you speak, try to only do so to ask more questions or to seek clarification on something you don't understand.
- Ask your friends of different ethnicities to recommend books, movies, TV shows, musicians, or documentaries that accurately capture their life experience and commit to watching or reading at least two.
- Invite a member of your congregation for dinner and ask them to share their experiences as a Caucasian/African American/Asian/Hispanic/Native American or whatever ethnicity with which they identify. Listen. Ask clarifying questions or ask them to expand on stories so you really understand. Ask about their experience in their community, at work, and in the church.

Chapter Four

BE SLOW TO TAKE OFFENSE

As IF WE HAVE a built-in emotional dashboard light indicating something is wrong, either internally (we're hurt, disappointed, afraid, etc.) or externally (from others' injustice, pain caused by loved ones, and so on), anger alerts us that something needs to change—either within or without.

People of every skin color are justifiably angry about hatred, violence, discrimination, and injustice. This righteous anger stems from a love of God and others. When we channel this anger toward action, dialogue, and internal change, we find ourselves working side by side with others who are trying to be part of the solution.

Sometimes, though, anger is like armor. We simply throw anger out in front of us defensively, frustrated that change isn't happening fast enough or aggravated that changes we've worked hard to make seem insignificant. We accuse. Justify. Shut down. When we use anger as a shield, as self-defense, it creates barriers to understanding. Relying on anger for protection or to persuade generally increases the level of conflict and often prolongs misunderstandings.

This kind of explosive anger may feel powerful, but it doesn't really protect; it deflects and destroys. Instead, Christians are to rely on the armor of God.

When we rely on God-given spiritual protection from those who seek to destroy us, rather than anger, we put on the following:

- truth as a belt to secure our center
- righteousness as a breastplate to protect our hearts
- the gospel as proper shoes mobilizing us to be where God wants us
- salvation as a helmet to protect our minds against Satan's attacks
- God's Word as our sword to fight the battle against evil
- faith as our shield against evil's intent (Ephesians 6:13–17)

God's armor creates openings for understanding and conversation.

When a young Israelite named David was about to fight an enemy soldier named Goliath, King Saul presented him with his personal armor. Like using anger as a defense, it would have seemed logical to people around him for David to use that armor. David, however, relied on God. Finding the king's armor made him clumsy and slow, he declined it in favor of his shield of faith. It must have looked like a foolish choice, but it was the wisest one. He defeated Goliath. Our choice to rely on God's armor may appear equally foolish, but it's still the wise choice.

God tells us to be like him, and he is slow to anger. Timothy Keller, in his sermon titled "The Healing of Anger," explains that what's biblical isn't "no anger or blow anger, but slow anger."[1] As we work through our stories, we agree to be slow to anger in order to fully hear one another. We admit we need salvation through the gospel of Jesus. We rely on Jesus's righteousness, not our own, and we commit to speak and hear truth. We offer our words in faith and trust God's Word over our own experience when the two are in conflict. This is how we rely on God's armor over our anger.

You may have felt anger at some of Saundra's experiences. And that's as it should be. God was angry too. Biblically expressed anger has its place in the face of injustice and hatred, but when engaging in conversations about race, it's wise to be *slow* to take offense.

If you are a person of color, you likely have experiences of your own to share. You may resonate with Lori's frustration that we're not as far along in the battle against racism as we imagined we'd be by now. If you're white, you may, like Lori, be intimidated by anger that feels directed at you when you've tried to be part of the solution.

What has been your experience with anger—both in setting it aside to rely on God's armor or in channeling it when it stems from love and motivates action?

WHAT CAN WE DO TO SLOW OUR ANGER?

Lori

None of my best friends are people of color. I may as well get that out of the way right now.

There's no racist agenda behind that; it's just how my life has panned out. I'm open to that changing.

I don't avoid people of color. I'm friendly with many. I worship, work, and relate (without incident and with joy) every day with people whose skin color is different from mine. Still, I have lived primarily in two small Rhode Island towns where most residents are white. I'm sure that impacts my perspective and my opportunities.

I want to write frankly here about being a white Christian living in these times. I suspect that many white readers have had experiences similar to mine, but we don't talk much about them for a lot of reasons. We wonder if our experiences have any worth. We feel some shame and responsibility that our culture isn't further along with racial healing. But we also feel frustration that our own contribution to be more loving and to promote appreciation across ethnicities seems to make so little difference. And the level of anger that accompanies most of the public rhetoric about race serves to silence us more than invite us into conversations of substance with people we don't know well.

Like many of you, I don't feel like a racist. Growing up in the sixties and seventies, I was raised on the concept of racial equality, being introduced to it by Mr. Rogers, the gang on *Sesame Street*, and Marlo

Thomas's *Free to Be . . . You and Me.* Living in a troubled home with absent or arguing parents, I never heard racist jokes or conversations around our table. But that may be because there was usually familial conflict instead. My cultural training was delivered through church, school, and television.

My church was Baptist and primarily white, but we worshiped regularly with the Baptist church from two towns over that was primarily black. I loved those combined services. I envied my black brothers and sisters their dynamic gospel preacher, interactive sermons (can I get an *Amen?*), vibrant music, and their practice of referring to fellow churchgoers as "Brother Everett" or "Sister Lucille" and so on.

I imagined that every black church had lively worship (sort of like a Tyler Perry movie marathon), and I envied that until, to my surprise, years later I visited a denomination of serious, somber black worshipers. Why I hadn't imagined there were variations in worship styles among people of color is evidence that I needed my experience expanded and my assumptions challenged.

My cultural training at school had a profound effect on me. Most students in our school were white or Native American. From elementary on we had guest speakers educating us on Narragansett Indian culture, the crimes of whites who had stolen the land, and the value of respecting people's unique histories. One of my earliest sorrows was that, as a white girl, I believed I had no rich culture and that my heritage was shame.

That's not something I discussed with other white people. I wonder if you had similar experiences? The anger that encompasses so many conversations about race and ethnicity makes it harder for anyone feeling shame or unworthiness to bring their experiences to the table, but that's what needs to occur. To say my whiteness hung heavy on me is an understatement.

I felt responsible not to repeat other generations' mistakes and to make amends. I admired Prudence Crandall. She was a white woman born in our hometown, the first teacher in America to open a school for black girls after her failed attempt to integrate them into her classroom. I had little real-life opportunity to act as she did.

So instead, I wrote papers on important black Americans for every school assignment. This was my first attempt to use words to make a difference—my earliest experiments of channeling anger into action and frustration into persuasion.

Of course, television was my generation's constant companion. We watched and listened to sitcoms and stand-up comedians as they modeled the use of humor to navigate social change and confront culture. We'd hoped and believed that racism was something that belonged to past generations. It's sad that we've lost touch with a willingness to laugh at ourselves. If hope deferred makes the heart sick, it appears justice deferred drains a society of humor.

I worked to have a heart open to all others, to see individuals, but it was complicated. In my twenties, I dated a black man who ended our relationship because he "could never be truly serious about a white woman." Then a Chinese friend for whom I developed feelings told me he could never marry someone not Asian. This was confusing and added to my feelings of shame about my whiteness.

These and other negative experiences based on skin color were unpleasant but were not permanently damaging. Like many other white people, I wanted desperately to be part of the solution but couldn't quite figure out how. I believe it's this frustration and confusion that can sometimes lead to defensive anger or a fear of failure that looks like apathy. The complexity of addressing racism can feel paralyzing, and there can appear to be no straight lines toward equality and freedom from racism.

Eventually I married a first-generation American with Dutch/Indonesian ancestry. We raised and homeschooled two children, teaching them to be loving and respectful of all people. While I believe racism is wrong and that we must love and honor all people, my focus has not been on racial activism but on working toward solutions via spiritual revolution. This choice is less about my fear of activism and more about my faith in the gospel to make lasting change.

Besides writing, I've always had a day job working with at-risk families. They come from all ethnicities and varied situations—some are from gated communities, others are homeless. Domestic violence, child abuse, mental health challenges, and substance abuse are no respecters of color or economic status.

I choose not to be color-blind; I don't act as if I don't recognize that a person with me is a different ethnicity or skin color from me. Besides feeling it's disingenuous, I want to acknowledge the whole person, and I appreciate variations in culture. Of course not all family cultures revolve around ancestry, but many do. As an adult, I've realized that I do indeed have a rich cultural background. However, my birth family's culture was more defined by my father's firefighting career than by skin color. My immediate family culture is largely defined by our faith. Families of all colors, I've learned, define individual cultures by more than their skin color or country of origin.

As a white person, awareness of racial tension isn't a part of my daily life. My overarching experience is that of shame. I've listened to stories of an elementary school boy who was called "the N-word" every day, and none of the teachers or staff were able, or possibly willing, to address it. I consider that shameful. I was thrilled that we had a black president, even if I don't agree with all of his politics. But then I heard a group of angry white young men turn our president's name into a curse word. I felt ashamed at my inability to change their hearts and minds.

> *Shame is also a silencer, and it impacts*
> *people of every color.*

And it's here that I think almost all of us can find ground to agree on. Shame—that powerful sense of humiliation—is never comfortable. In *Psychology Today*, Dr. Andrea Brandt says, "When we harbor shame, we tend to react defensively when we're criticized or given even mild feedback."[2] As believers, it can be freeing to admit to feelings of shame rather than resorting to covering them with anger or avoidance of the topic.

Shame is also a silencer, and it impacts people of every color. The anger that encompasses so many conversations about race and ethnicity makes it harder for anyone feeling shame or unworthiness to engage in productive dialogue.

During a visit to a primarily black church gathering, I listened as older folk told stories of racism they'd experienced over the years. Someone remarked about the progress we've made, and people exchanged glances. "It's still there," said one of the older men. "It's gone underground a bit, but it lurks in the darkness, waiting." Shame hung in the air.

One of my former pastors once looked out over our small congregation and announced that initially, he was disappointed to see such a white congregation, but over the weeks, he'd happily discovered we also have congregants from Nigeria, Venezuela, India, and the Philippines. My goal is inclusion, too, but it's strange to feel like a disappointment, ashamed of something I can't change. This feeling of shame sparked momentary anger. But I inhaled and processed it. On one level, I get it. On another level, I wonder if there wasn't another way to express the desire to welcome all ethnicities. Perhaps he was fighting his own shame.

Despite decades of education, social awareness, sitcoms, and stand-up routines, as I face my sixties, hatred haunts our nation. I no longer operate from guilt, having made peace with God for my design. I've sorrowed over sins of previous generations and have searched my heart to be part of the solution. Racial division, especially in some regions, seems insurmountable. And yet.

My worldview is embedded in God's Word. It's there that I first learned that hatred and racism are sins. The only way out of bondage is Jesus. So now, as always, this is where my hope lies—in the gospel, redemption, sanctification by the Holy Spirit, and the fellowship of believers.

A while back, I spoke at a convention for a Protestant denomination. Not only was there an array of skin colors in attendance, but there was also an intentional design for inclusivity during the week. Featured speakers were a balanced mix of black, Hispanic, and white preachers. Worship music was a combination of traditional/gospel/contemporary and wasn't always in English. There were ongoing opportunities for all people to weigh in on how the denomination could improve relationships and in respecting cultures. The week's theme was the courage to have hard conversations, be slow to anger, and to act on the gospel. Disagreement was expected and was navigated well.

At mealtimes, there were still long tables where only one skin color was represented, but there were also tables where blacks, whites, and Hispanics mingled. It was clear there were deep, easy friendships between individuals of diverse backgrounds. People shared food and laughter.

Here there was hope. There was more work to be done, more conversations to be had. But hope. No matter how hard the work, we can't give up.

This is my entry point into activism. To offer my failed hopes, pathetic efforts, blind spots, listening ear, and my experience with hard conversations. To work from within the body of Christ through which I believe his light shines. To be undaunted by being a sixty-something white woman with little to contribute. That's fine. Whatever I have, I offer with love in the resistance against hatred, fear, misunderstanding, racism, and violence.

I believe God. He says that if one suffers, we all suffer. By confessing shame, by being slow to anger, and by truly talking, through the power of Christ, we can heal and create a future where we rise together.

Saundra

Assumptions can be dangerous. I did not realize how many things I had assumed about Lori just from superficial experiences we have had in the past. I was not surprised to hear that none of her best friends are black. This is something I assumed, considering the racial composition of Rhode Island is 80 percent white and less than 7 percent black. What I did not expect was to find out Lori had attended predominantly black church services in the past or that she had been in various interracial relationships. This showed an openness to experience cultures outside of how she grew up and excited me about the possibility of where our conversation could go over the course of writing this book together.

One of my greatest fears about stepping into this conversation is to get deep into a topic where we do not have enough shared life experience to deal with the various aspects of that topic. In looking at both of our experiences, this will not be the case. We have both experienced what it feels like to be rejected in relationships due to our cultural background. We have both wrestled with identity. We have both had times in our lives where we let stereotyping and bias speak louder than the truth of God's word. We have both had times when we have failed to love through the eyes of Jesus, and I suspect you have too.

Our fear of what we will find when we dive into these hard conversations is part of the problem. I do not believe most people are racist. But even if we were not the ones saying the words, inflicting the pain directly, or doing any of these things that are overtly racist, our inaction adds to the toxicity. By not doing anything, not saying anything, and acting as if racism does not exist, we become a part of the problem because we will not engage and become part of the solution.

The challenge for every believer is to no longer see ourselves as having too little to contribute. To no longer diminish our own significance or devalue our circle of influence, regardless of its size. To be like David looking at a giant with eyes of possibility. Laying down our expectation of what we can do in our own strength and link arms with heaven. To move into a mindset that believes one can put a thousand to flight and two can put ten thousand to flight. Where our collective efforts help to eradicate racial injustice and encourage diversity in the unique way that we each are designed by God to share his love, light, and truth in the world. Learning Lori's assumptions about black church services made me recall the first time I took a white friend to my all-black church. We were a group of believers who danced like David did, loud and unashamedly lifting our highest praise.

Amid clapping hands and swaying to the beat, she leaned over to whisper in my ear, "This must be what it feels like to be free." That night we chatted about the experience and about feeling free enough to dance before the Lord. In that moment of worship, she released the discomfort of being the only white person in the congregation and clung to the presence of God. Isn't that the goal of every church service, to help people encounter God? I always wonder how many opportunities we miss encountering God in new ways due to lack of variety of cultural expressions within our Sunday services. Loud praising and quiet reflection are both ways to the cross. Neither is right or wrong; they are just different.

Even with a desire to see more spiritual diversity within churches, it stung to hear Lori's portrayal of the pastor's disappointment of seeing only white faces, leaving her "feeling like a disappointment for something I can't change." It took me a moment to realize why these words hung heavy in my heart after reading them. This sentence shares what so many people of color feel every day, prejudice for something we cannot change and that others do not want to change. Rather than disappointment, the expression we are sometimes met with is distrust, disdain, or dismissal. Unfortunately, those feelings often move beyond facial expressions and into action.

When reading about Lori's experience in the grocery store with a bill thought to be counterfeit, it made me think about the similarities between a recent example with a black person that ended in a vastly different way. It is helpful, whenever we hear about these types of situations with officers, to take into consideration all the facts surrounding the case.

> *Justice becomes skewed when we do not have hard conversations about race, unconscious bias, and systemic racism.*

But at no time do I feel it is warranted to assume a greater likelihood of guilt due to an abundance of melanin in someone's skin tone or to assume innocence for the lack thereof. Guilt should be proven beyond a reasonable doubt. That is the hallmark of justice within our country. It's what every juror agrees to achieve when selected. They vow to take an unbiased look at the evidence presented to them. They agree to move past their own beliefs about a situation to rely solely on the concrete evidence placed before them. Yet long before an official trial has been conducted for many, the initial decision of innocence and guilt is made off their first impression, based on surface evidence. This is what saddens my heart. Justice becomes skewed when we do not have hard conversations about race, unconscious bias, and systemic racism.

There are a host of potential responses to the unjust action of others—everything from ignoring it to full-scale war. But it's important to remember that God is a God of justice. While he expects us to respond to injustice in a measured way, he is the only one who can put things back into right standing, through his righteousness and holiness. He alone can judge the sin and iniquity of the world rightly. His justice is mitigated by his love and mercy toward us. We also have governing bodies within the world who do this to the best of their human ability. Our human limitations make it even more important that we begin from a place of love and evaluate our own heart toward the presumed guilty to allow room for justice.

I was intrigued by the conversation Lori overheard—they were discussing race within our nation—where one of the gentlemen stated, "it's gone underground a bit, but it lurks in the darkness, waiting." There is some truth in this statement regarding racism in America. It is like an abscess festering in the dark recesses of our culture that is covered up with outer dressing to make it look appealing to the eye. But underneath, the toxicity remains. Every now and then something happens to poke at the wound.

An unarmed black person is killed in a traffic stop with questionable surrounding circumstances. Someone is picked for a position over a more qualified person of color. Someone slings a racial slur as a way of releasing their frustration. Each incident pushes on the wound until, eventually, we begin to see the toxicity spewing out and the infection spreads. It spread to the restaurant table where Lori overheard the twenty-somethings ranting about President Obama, but even more importantly, it also spreads to the dinner table of hundreds of homes, where it is spoken behind closed doors. This is how it remains in the darkness, waiting.

For any wound to truly heal it must have a time of radical debridement. The diseased, unhealthy part needs either to be cleansed or removed to allow the healthy tissue to thrive. In the same way, we must identify those in authority who need greater diversity training or need to be removed from their position of leadership in order to prevent further cultural disease.

I agree with Lori's synopsis. There are many helpful, supportive, caring police officers in the world who do not deserve to be shot and ambushed in their cars because of the pain someone feels about the racial injustice inflicted by another. There is no good reason for anyone to hurt someone else. But as the adage goes, "hurt people hurt people." It is what happens when toxicity is not healed—it replicates. As the story Lori shared of the young gentleman hearing derogatory words at school demonstrated, many of those who are doing these acts are punching back because they feel those who are supposed to stand up for them have not done so. They take matters into their own hands, anger numbing the pain, even if only for a moment.

During those times of emotional pain, we need to take a step back to reflect. Only then can the fruit of self-control have room to flow within our conversations. Being slow to anger requires practice on the training ground of hard conversations and past battles. How I communicate grace to those I encounter is different from Lori and is probably different from you too. How I relate to the world is framed by my experiences. Those experiences are infused with the flavor I bring when I show up in the room and carry over into the melody I sing when I worship. Everything that makes me who I am, the uniqueness of my personal design, is necessary for God's greater plan in my life. The same is true for Lori and the same is true about you. And that's as it should be.

There is one sentence from Lori that gave me the greatest hope—"I choose not to be color-blind."

I have had many well-meaning white friends tell me they are color-blind. They share how they don't see color, they just see people. This always feels disingenuous to me. It is impossible to look at me and not notice the color of my skin.

In fact, I prefer you choose *not* to be color-blind. See the color and embrace the cultural differences. Choose to open not only your eyes but also your mind and your heart. Choose to receive everything that makes me who I am, as I receive everything that makes you who you are. This is how we grow. This is how we learn. This is how we heal. Together with our eyes wide open.

At no time during this conversation do I want Lori's whiteness to weigh heavy on her or your ethnicity to burden you. Instead, I ask you all to place your whiteness, your brownness, your blackness beside my blackness and see Jesus loving us all equally. Then we can take up the robe of his righteousness together and allow it to adorn each other, allowing us the grace to speak freely and to extend mercy when the words may not come easily. As we navigate these hard conversations, we can cast off protective reactions and rise together to a new place of understanding and unity.

COLORFUL CONVERSATION WITH DORINA LAZO GILMORE-YOUNG

I come from a multiracial heritage. My mom's family is predominantly Italian and a little bit Jewish. My dad's family is mostly Filipino, but also Chinese, Indian, Polynesian, and African. My parents raised us to celebrate the diversity of all the different parts of our cultures and our background.

Because I am a person of color, I had to reckon with my cultural identity. I would say probably in college was the time when I really felt most strongly that I was a minority. I went to an elementary school and a high school on Chicago's South Side that were very culturally diverse. It wasn't until I attended a college that was 96 percent white with only 4 percent of us being people of color that I thought, *This feels really different.* Even just walking around, everybody knew who I was because I looked different. In classes and during conversations, I realized my cultural identity wasn't necessarily something that people recognized or celebrated in the same way that I had experienced as a young person in Chicago. This was also the time when I felt called by God to be a bridge to help other friends think about racial issues. I enjoyed being in several classes where we talked about the sociology of race and current events.

After college, I remember talking about some current events with a roommate. I don't recall the entire conversation, but I remember her saying, "Why are you so passionate about this? I just consider you to be a white girl." I didn't realize in that moment how hard and hurtful that was for me because she didn't realize that I was a person of color from a mixed-race background.

Quite frankly, it shouldn't have mattered. There should have been a sensitivity, no matter what. But her assumption was that only people of color should care about racial issues, and she just considered me white, which she thought was benevolent. That conversation stuck with me. I mean, this is decades later, and I'm still thinking about that comment.

This is one of the challenges, especially for mixed race individuals. Sometimes people don't recognize your background or recognize that a comment can be hurtful. I think it goes to the idea some people have that it's a good thing to be color-blind and not to acknowledge somebody's racial heritage. That communicates: I don't see you. I don't recognize that part of who you are. I think that's why the conversation was so hurtful to me. But I didn't have the language to articulate that in the moment, or to challenge her comments. I just let it go. I internalized it, and it hurt me.

Now I realize that's not the best way to have a conversation, because it's not truly having honest dialogue. I should have explained to her why the comment was hurtful, that my cultural heritage is something that's really important to me. Her dismissing it felt like her not seeing and loving me as a person. If I could redo that conversation, I would have challenged her a little bit more. I would have at least asked a question like, "What do you mean by that exactly? Do you know what my heritage is? Do you know what my background is?" I might even have gone a step further and talked about how we are all image-bearers of God, and how it's our job to protect other people regardless of their race, culture, or skin color.

DORINA LAZO GILMORE-YOUNG is an author, speaker, Bible teacher, and podcaster. Her ethnicity is Filipino, Italian, Chinese, Polynesian, Indian, African, and Jewish.

STEP 4: BE SLOW TO TAKE OFFENSE.

When we agree to have a hard conversation, it's vital that we also agree to obey God in being slow to take offense. This can seem like a tall order to fill, but we have the supreme example of Jesus Christ.

He created a beautiful world for us and designed us to worship his father. When Jesus walked among us, he had every reason to take offense every moment of every day; and yet he was a person sinners welcomed to their tables. He is the reason we have hope that we can be offended and yet remain in the conversation. We are to be slow to take offense, and we are also to be forgiving, full of grace and mercy, as he is, and yet still provide guidance and correction. These guardrails should provide the support for hard conversations so that there is freedom.

> *We need to use discernment when we listen*
> *to people expressing anger, and consider if*
> *what they're expressing stems from an unjust*
> *condition that rightly needs to be addressed.*

Jesus did, at times, express righteous anger, such as when he confronted the Pharisees or when he ejected the money changers from the temple. We need to use discernment when we listen to people expressing anger, and consider if what they're expressing stems from an unjust condition that rightly needs to be addressed. These considerations call for wisdom, but God promises to provide when we ask.

It can help, even when talking with just one other person, to begin by agreeing to not only be open and honest but also to hear one another with love, to be slow to take offense, and to be quick to repent—and then to offer forgiveness. With these ground rules, we can make great progress together.

Scripture

Philippians 2 tells us Jesus emptied himself and became a servant. He humbled himself, even to the point of death on the cross. Likewise, we're to "do nothing from selfish ambition or conceit, but in humility count others more significant than yourselves. Let each of you look not only to his own interests, but also to the interests of others" (Philippians 2:3–4). So in conversations about race, we are wise and Christlike to commit to being slow to anger.

In chapter 3 we referenced verse 19 of James 1. Now consider that verse along with the end of James's sentence, which he completed in verse 20: "Know this, my beloved brothers: let every person be quick to hear, slow to speak, slow to anger; for the anger of man does not produce the righteousness of God." Also consider Proverbs 19:11: "Good sense makes one slow to anger, and it is his glory to overlook an offense."

What does being slow to anger look like in practice? What difference could it make in this whole conversation about race?

In what ways would being slow to anger encourage more people to be willing to share their stories or their thoughts? How might we benefit if more individuals participated in this conversation toward healing?

Starting Places

- Commit to being slow to anger. Ask God to help you see when you are taking offense or becoming defensive.

- Research Bible verses about being slow to anger or slow to take offense. Write the verses that really speak to you on index cards or Post-it Notes, and keep them somewhere handy so you can meditate on these biblical instructions.
- If you catch yourself taking offense or speaking from anger, stop speaking. Pause. Apologize for taking offense and ask to reset the conversation. Ask the other person to explain, again, their perspective and commit to hearing them out. Respond with questions and clarifications before you share your own perspective.

Chapter Five

SEEK A BETTER WAY TO LOVE

Scripture is clear. We must all learn to love. Without it, we're nothing more than annoying, loud, clanging cymbals.

In fact, without love, we miss the whole point (1 Corinthians 13).

But how do we love well? It's helpful to recognize that God is love, so he's how we measure if we're loving others well or not. The Corinthians 13 passage is useful because it has concrete instructions about how to know if we're loving someone. Are we being patient and kind? Are we refraining from envy and boasting? Are we being arrogant or rude, insisting on our own way and indulging irritability and resentfulness? Do we refrain from rejoicing at wrongdoing, instead always choosing to rejoice with the truth? Are we willing to bear all things, believe all things, hope all things, and endure all things? Before we claim to love others who are different from us, it's wise to prayerfully meditate on our actions in light of this passage.

So in Christ, we learn to love others in general, but it's also vital, when loving individuals specifically, to listen to how they *receive* love. What looks like love to me may not look like love to someone else. When we reach across cultures or ethnic differences, asking questions about how people experience, express, and receive love is important, and it may be different family to family, community to community, and individual to individual. As you read this chapter, consider how you feel loved as well as how you express it.

IN WHAT WAYS CAN I ACTIVELY EXPRESS GOD'S LOVE FOR OTHERS?

Saundra

Every September my family and I make sure we have a collection of maroon-colored T-shirts and hoodies available to wear. We know that for the next twelve Fridays at 7 p.m., we will be surrounded by other maroon-wearing family, friends, and students cheering on the local high school football team.

On this night, we arrived early enough to watch our team warm up on the field. My oldest son is the starting defensive end and was busy stretching his calf muscles in preparation for two hours of running the field. He was pumped up and ready for a night of hitting, blocking, and if all went well, stopping the opposing team from racking up points. The ninety-degree-plus blistering heat of Alabama was still evident, even as the sun began to go down.

Within moments of the final verse of "The Star-Spangled Banner," we kicked off to the opposing team. On the left and right of me were families of every ethnicity. Most of those surrounding me wore our high school's colors. Others waved pom poms or flags to testify of their allegiance to the team. Suddenly, during one possession of the ball, a player on the opposing team hit our kicker after a punt. The young man on the ground became the son of every football mama on our team. His mother did not have to say a word, because every mama jumped up yelling. A bad call on one of your kids is a bad call on all our kids. We were a collective body of football mamas defending our own. We even have the T-shirts to prove it. Yes, actual T-shirts that say our high school's name and the words FOOTBALL MAMA.

As the game progressed throughout the night, our team established a slim lead. Each of the opposing team's snaps had us on our feet yelling at our defense to "Hold that line!" It was critical not to allow the opponent to get another first down.

The scoreboard showed fourth down with one yard to go. The ball sailed from the center to the quarterback, and as he was about to throw it down the field to his intended target on the 10-yard line, my son brought him to the ground. The roar that erupted from our side was deafening. We were three victory formations away from another check in the win column.

Our behavior during sporting games can teach us a lot about how prejudice and bias work, specifically as it relates to social identity theory. This theory states that we get some of our sense of personal self-worth from the groups we belong to. These groups include everything from the neighborhood you live in, the school you graduated from, your ethnicity, your sex, or anything that can be used to define you. These associations can become a part of your sense of self-esteem. So when the groups we associate with do well, we feel better about ourselves. There is a collective uplifting associated with identifying with a group that is thriving.

We see this in effect at sporting events. You show up wearing your team's colors and waving their flag. Every time the ref makes a bad call, it almost feels personal. Our ability to self-identify with our sports teams can have complete strangers celebrating over a win and for a moment completely forgetting about any other differences that may exist. During those moments, our own personal feelings of pride and worth are bolstered by the success of the team with which we identify. Despite having no direct part in the actual game or playing a part in the win, you may find yourself yelling "We won!" This is what social identity theory looks like, and it is active in other areas of our life.

Self-identification with a group positions us for bias. We will argue with those on the opposing team. We will defend the actions of our players. And in this situation, we experience the freedom to express our bias. But once all the tailgating has ended and our foam fingers are packed in the attic, then we are forced to re-evaluate our current social identity groups. Those groups will often fall into more cultural, ethnic, or socioeconomic categories.

On the other side of social identity theory are those groups that we do not belong to and do not see as part of our personal identity. These groups are outside of our personal realm of interaction and are often unfamiliar to us. This can sometimes be viewed as in-groups and out-groups.

In-groups are those collections of individuals with whom you have something in common. Out-groups are those collections of individuals with whom you do not have something in common. Because of the positive emotions we experience when the groups we identify with are winning, thriving, and succeeding, it can inadvertently cause us to live life with an us-versus-them mentality.

You have been there. You're in a room full of people, most of whom are one race that is not yours. Upon looking around, you finally identify someone who looks like you. Instantly you feel a connection with this person without knowing a thing about them.

You may have experienced this in other social situations where you meet a group of new people who are all your ethnicity, and you find out one of them graduated from the same college as you. A new in-group is formed, and you will find yourself more drawn to this person than the others, who you do not immediately identify with as part of your in-group. This in-grouping can be seen among religious groups and in any situation where people can self-identify.

It is important to understand how our mind works and the intentionality required to love like Jesus. It takes work to love the way Jesus calls us to love.

Since we are one of many within our in-groups, we have more opportunities to spend time with various people within those groups. We are better able to differentiate group members by their unique personalities and characteristics. Because we do not immediately have connections with those in our out-groups, we have fewer opportunities to engage one-on-one with these individuals and have a greater tendency to stereotype members of those out-groups based on our limited exposure to a select few in those out-groups. This "us and them" mentality is often the starting point where prejudice and discrimination can begin. The contrast to in-group favoritism is out-group negativity, or a desire for your groups to always be in a more favorable position than another group.

We can begin to favor those in our in-groups without intentionally trying to exhibit bias or prejudice toward those in our out-groups simply because of how we feel when our in-groups are doing well. Therefore, it is important to understand how our mind works and the intentionality required to love like Jesus. It takes work to love the way Jesus calls us to love.

One of the best examples of this is shown in Luke 10. Jesus shares this story in reply to a young man who asked the question, who is my neighbor? Who is the person you have called me to love as myself?

> A man was going down from Jerusalem to Jericho, when he was attacked by robbers. They stripped him of his clothes, beat him and went away, leaving him half dead. A priest happened to be going down the same road, and when he saw the man, he passed by on the other side. So too, a Levite, when he came to the place and saw him, passed by on the other side. But a Samaritan, as he traveled, came where the man was; and when he saw him, he took pity on him. He went to him and bandaged his wounds, pouring on oil and wine. Then he put the man on his own donkey, brought him to an inn and took care of him. The next day he took out two denarii and gave them to the innkeeper. "Look after him," he said, "and when I return, I will reimburse you for any extra expense you may have." (Luke 10:30–35 NIV)

In this story, we can see the inner working of in-groups and out-groups, as well as how love can transcend this psychological process. We can immediately identify the robbers as an out-group. No one wants to be associated with being an active participant in harming another. However, looking at this passage as a person of faith, we may self-identify with the priest or the Levite based on religious common ground. Yet we do not want to self-identify with the fact that their inactivity is just as harmful as the activity of the robbers. In doing nothing, they are neglecting this person by leaving him without having helped.

In contrast, the Samaritan does not respond based on what group the injured person falls within but on what is the best way to show love to the person in his current state. He bandaged his wounds, lavished the injured man with care, and promised to return to check on him. This is what it looks like to show love to people of other ethnicities. It is an intentional form of love that does not inflict further injury by doing nothing, but steps into the healing equation.

When asked, "'Which of these three do you think was a neighbor to the man who fell into the hands of robbers?' The expert in the law replied, 'The one who had mercy on him.' Jesus told him, 'Go and do likewise'" (Luke 10:36–37 NIV).

Lori

Loving others is a calling most of us take seriously. Still, we fail at loving up to biblical standards all the time. I'm still learning to love Jesus after more than sixty years of following him, and still learning to love my husband well into our fourth decade of loving. Learning to love other Christians, those outside of the faith, and the diverse range of people God created will take my entire life. But I can't use that overarching reality to be an excuse for not investing specific effort in loving those who look different from me.

I also can't think of loving people different from me as something I attempt only after I've gotten good at loving those closest to, or most like, me. In fact, it's an illusion that those nearest and dearest are like me. God is so very different from me by virtue of being God, but I have responded by loving him. Of all the men I'd ever met, I thought my husband was most like me, but within the first few years of marriage, vast differences appeared. Yet we love across the gap.

So this act of reaching out and loving someone unlike me isn't totally foreign. But continuing to love someone once we know them better and differences emerge is different from learning to love when our differences announce themselves from across the room. Skin color and cultural differences are often immediately apparent. We can let that be a barrier to initial engagement, or we can remember that all love takes time and effort, whether that's the initial effort of seeing past differences or discovering them as we go.

> *Jesus calls us to love now, not when we think we're ready or when we believe we're capable or when it's convenient.*

The enticing truth about the effort to love is that the skills learned in one area are applicable across a range of relationships. Furthermore, Jesus calls us to love now, not when we think we're ready or when we believe we're capable or when it's convenient. If we want to be where he is at work, we must be present where he is working now.

Since my youth, the first step to loving people from other cultural backgrounds has meant listening to their stories and believing their experiences. It's not always easy or pain free. I remember a woman from the local Narragansett Tribe in Rhode Island, Princess Redwing, speaking to my seventh-grade class about the stories of her people. She was mesmerizing, and her stories captured my heart.

Once she concluded her storytelling, a gentleman from the tribe then shared some of the history of conflict between Native Americans and white settlers. His historical descriptions of massacres and betrayals were devastating in their detail. He went on to explain ongoing conflicts in our time. His words landed heavy on my young heart, and I cried for several nights alone in my room, wishing I could erase this painful history for Princess Redwing and her people or some-how change my own skin color so as not to be associated with such atrocities.

The gentleman used the phrase "white oppressors" over and over until it rang in my ears. I didn't feel like a white oppressor at age eleven and didn't want any part of that story to play out in my own life. It startles me every time I read Saundra's use of the words *oppressor* and *oppressed*. I've never entered a friendship from this angle. I don't identify as an oppressor. I get it, but it's still a word over which I must climb to continue our conversation and deepen my commitment to being open.

Over the years, my sorrow over Princess Redwing and others like her have made me deeply conscious that there are other white people like me who care about learning to love and who don't believe they have special rights and privileges by virtue of their skin color. Many of us don't want to be part of the problem, even as we admit that we may have blind spots and important love lessons to learn. Loving me means understanding that I can't possibly carry the crime of every white person on my shoulders and survive. It means understanding that I want to cultivate a cultural humility because it's biblical, but that I can no more change the color of my skin or the history of our people than you can.

I had several reactions while reading Saundra's opening for this chapter. The first regards football. Being from New England, I've experienced the joy of being a fan of a champion team, the New England Patriots. I used to joke that my children are so self-confident because they grew up in the age of winning New England sports teams—Patriots, Red Sox, Celtics, and Boston Bruins.

As a Patriots fan, I also know what it's like to be hated simply for my association with a team that dominated so many Super Bowls. Whenever the Patriots were down, I would invariably receive texts from friends around the country, not commiserating but gloating and wishing a loss for my team. Normally, these friends would look for every opportunity to build me up, but in the world of football, I became fair game because my team was on top.

During the Patriots' losing season of 2020, instead of kind support, I received comments like "It's about time" and "Now you know how it feels." The strange dynamics of identification by association. Of course, unlike skin color, I can transfer my allegiance to another team (as did some New Englanders who began cheering for Tampa Bay when quarterback Tom Brady left the Patriots to play for the Tampa Bay Buccaneers), but it's interesting how identification with a group can impact a person's sense of self or other people's thoughts about the person.

The second reaction I had was in relation to this statement by Saundra: "You have been there. You are in a room full of people, most of whom are one race that is not yours." You know you haven't grown up as a minority when you have to think hard about times when you've walked into a room where all are of one race that isn't your own. It hasn't been a common experience for me.

In fact, in high school I tried to understand what it's like to be surrounded by people of different ethnicity, so I pulled a copy of *Ebony* magazine off the library shelf and slowly thumbed through the pages. It was an odd feeling to turn page after page and see only people of color, but for me, it was instructive, and the memory of that experience remains sharp in my mind even more than forty years later.

Through the years, I've tried to experience and understand other cultures, whether it was the culture of the black church in the next town over or the Japanese church to which I was assigned for summer missions. I once tried to express appreciation to the mother of the house where I was staying in Japan by bringing her a small bouquet of flowers. To my horror, she burst into tears, and the older son explained that I had offered her flowers intended to be offered to deceased ancestors. I was reminded how important it is not to assume what love looks like to another person.

At that denominational conference where I was a speaker and appreciated the clear efforts at inclusion and diversity, I admit I battled my internal overthinking monologue whenever I entered the dining hall. As a speaker, I knew I would likely be welcome at any table, but still I hesitated to plop my tray down at one of the long tables filled primarily with either black or Hispanic faces.

It had nothing to do with my lack of desire to eat with nonwhites but was caused by my insecurities and probably an element of spiritual warfare. I battled thoughts like, *Will they perceive this as me joining them, or will it seem like a white person trying to demonstrate how fine I am for being the only white person at their table?* or *Have they chosen not to sit with white people because they don't want to sit with white people, and I'd be intruding?* I could have been intruding at the tables of the white people, too, but that wasn't even a thought when approaching them.

I'll admit I usually resolved the dilemma by looking for the integrated tables and eating there. I never did muster the nerve I believed it would take simply to ask if they would mind my joining them. I feel bad about my hesitation to this day. It would have helped if someone had invited me, but they may not have wanted to risk rejection, or they may have been just too busy enjoying fellowship to notice me hovering nearby. Sometimes overthinking and too much focus on self interfere with simple acts of love.

Because there have been years and years of whites dominating the conversation, I'm happy to see other voices become prominent and take positions of leadership. I applaud the inclusivity and would be concerned to find myself in an important policy meeting with all white faces, because we serve a broader demographic. I don't respond this way because I'm politically correct; I do it in response to God's call to love my neighbor. At the same time, I appreciate it when others refrain from making insensitive remarks about "old white men," or ask, "Do white people even have a culture?" I notice when people are careful to be respectful, kind, and loving to everyone in the room without showing favoritism based on skin color or race. This sort of common kindness makes getting to know one another and learning to love across differences much easier!

I understand Saundra's frustration when white people come to her to ask for ideas about how to do better. Maybe it's like the frustration I experienced early in my marriage whenever I felt my husband was neglecting me or not loving me well. Inevitably he would ask, "What exactly do you want? Just tell me and I will do it." I resisted that because it felt artificial. I have this innate desire for him to do the work of observing, listening, paying attention, and seeking God on my behalf to discover the ways that I feel loved. And I do believe that's important. But I've also learned that one way I can love my husband is to show him the mercy of sometimes just stating my needs simply in a straightforward, noncondemning manner and by not making him feel foolish for asking. He and I are in this marriage together, and we try to deal with our interpersonal challenges cooperatively.

> *Working together is hard, but Christians do hard things.*

Similarly, we are all trying to address the imbalances, the consequences, and the heartache of racism and cultural insensitivity together. Much of the solution to the issues we discuss in this book comes down to loving one another better than our ancestors did and better than we did yesterday and the day before.

Working together is hard, but Christians do hard things.

I think ahead to the day when we are all before the great throne of heaven, worshiping with people of every tribe, tongue, and nation. Jesus is all that will matter, and we will see how united we are in him. On that day, I will no longer fear people associating me with white supremacists or hate groups because my skin is white. Saundra will no longer fear that her sons will be in harm's way simply because their skin is brown. We will inhabit God's idea of us when he created us, and we will be filled with and surrounded by love.

What's imperative now is that Christians unite in our purpose so that our generation, people of all ethnicities, receive the gospel and have every opportunity to stand with us on that day. Love for Jesus and for those yet to know him should motivate us to set every barrier aside and find our way to mutual love. Love is our shibboleth, the code that sets Jesus followers apart from others. Loving others distinguishes us as "a chosen race, a royal priesthood, a holy nation, a people for his own possession, that you may proclaim the excellencies of him who called you out of darkness into his marvelous light" (1 Peter 2:9).

This work is daunting, uncomfortable, and humbling, but He is worthy of every effort. Let love for him fortify us to love one another.

COLORFUL CONVERSATION WITH MARIA GILL

I'm a Filipina. I'm also part Spanish because of my great-grandma and great-grandpa during the Spanish colonization. Growing up, I always compared myself to my sisters, who have a lighter skin tone than I do. I would hear people rank who was the most beautiful among us three sisters. I was always the last one because I'm the darkest. That was just the way it was. Even now a lot of people think that the fairer skin you have, the prettier you are—the more beautiful you are. In the Philippines, there are a lot of whitening products for the skin. So when I got to the United States, it was the opposite of the Philippines; there are a lot of tanning products available. It was funny to see the differences. It took me a while to get over thinking dark skin is not as beautiful as fair skin.

But my mom would always say to appreciate your natural beauty (the way God made you) or to appreciate the person he made you to be.

My husband is Caucasian, and I've been blessed with in-laws who openly embrace me. They are genuinely interested in my culture. Gatherings are an opportunity for me to share about where I came from and to educate them. I tell them what people are like in the Philippines. I share about lifestyle, arts, and mostly general differences. I explain to them things like: in the Philippines you have to put the right or left hand of the elderly on your forehead as an offering of blessing. In fact, when my husband went with me to the Philippines the very first time, he did not know that you should only bless the elderly. He was blessing everyone, even the little children.

As a mom, I have seen my son deal with skin tone as well. He had an incident where someone in his class was picking on him for being brown. I explained to him that this kid could have heard the derogatory word he used from his family or TV. We have to understand what's in the heart of this person. What's the intention?

I don't want my son to be bothered by this incident because we have to embrace whatever skin we're in. We have to be kind to one another and loving. I told him, "You have to be proud of who you are, and what matters is what's in your heart." We have always had open conversations with him. We have talked to him as adults who are experienced with conversations such as this because he needs to be able to deal with these situations like an adult.

I feel for parents like us who are going through this process. You want to protect your children. But I wouldn't want to enclose our son in a box. I think it is important to introduce kids to difficult conversations about race and skin color. It's important to teach them to welcome, learn about, and enjoy different cultures. We each make connections in different ways, as long as we're open to it.

MARIA GIL is a Jesus-following wife, mother, church secretary, and worship leader in Rhode Island. She is a proud citizen of her adopted country, America. Her ethnicity is Filipino.

STEP 5: SEEK CONCRETE WAYS TO LOVE PEOPLE OF DIFFERENT SKIN COLORS.

Look for ways to love people no matter what their skin color. Everyone has a different love language, and it's dictated by personality, temperament, age, culture, and faith as much as by ethnicity.

Ask questions. Seek relationships with people of every ethnicity, and ask how they are most likely to feel loved and valued in a relationship, in church, and in your community. Believe what they say and act on it. It's so important not to assume anything about how people feel loved based on their ethnicity or on our own experience.

When getting to know someone, we may offer choices about getting together—would it be more comfortable for us to meet at my home, your home, or a local restaurant? When discussing worship, we can ask if individuals feel their worship culture is reflected in our corporate worship rather than assuming discomfort because they are a cultural minority. Worship cultures are as different as ethnic or geographic cultures, and that is something Scripture welcomes.

Scripture

At the last supper, Jesus said, "A new commandment I give to you, that you love one another; as I have loved you, that you also love one another" (John 13:34 NKJV). It's powerful to know that God believes we not only need a relationship with him but also with one another. Reflect on 1 John 4:20–21, "If someone says, 'I love God,' and hates his brother, he is a liar; for he who does not love his brother whom he has seen, how can he love God whom he has not seen? And this commandment we have from Him: that he who loves God *must* love his brother also" (NKJV).

What are some ways you have felt loved by people of other ethnicities or cultures?

What are some ways you have learned to love people who are different from you?

Why do you think the Bible teaches that it's inconsistent to say that we love God while hating our brother or sister?

Starting Places

- It can be uncomfortable for people to explain how they want to be loved. Ask any spouse! Listen. Observe. Then do something loving. Take the risk of being misunderstood in order to love.

- Your church or small group could create a "How to Love Me" tree in the foyer. Using a paper tree or a real one, provide a variety of paper and markers. Ask people to trace around their hands (or feet!) and cut them out. Have some hearts precut for people who don't want to trace and cut. Encourage them then to write one way people could love them that would touch their hearts. Ask them to sign their name. Add their hand or foot or heart to the tree. Find a time to read them aloud and to commit to loving one another better and better all the time.

- Seek out a local group making headlines in your community—protesters, police, advocates, young people, politicians, a tribe, a victimized group, an angry group. Commit to pray for them. Invite their leaders in for a time when your church community just listens to their hearts. Ask how the church can pray for them, and try to find one concrete action the church can take to show them love. It's not essential (or even sometimes possible) to find a place of agreement between the church and this group. Just look to demonstrate God's love in some concrete way.

Chapter Six

RESIST THE TEMPTATION OF CANCEL CULTURE

GOD'S COMMAND FOR CHRISTIANS to bear with one another in love can be especially challenging in today's culture. In both Ephesians 4:2 and Colossians 3:13, God instructs us to forgive one another, bear with one another, and to do so with humility and gentleness. In the heated rhetoric of our times, Christians have an opportunity to be radically countercultural. Bearing with one another flies in the face of what we've come to know as "cancel culture."

Cancel culture starts when a large group of people boycott, criticize, or publicly reject a public figure for stating ideas that go against the current standards of that community. But it is also something done on a smaller scale—working to eliminate anyone's voice who doesn't fit the publicly accepted standard. It's like cultural shunning. For example, if a comedienne makes public comments deemed racist, people may demand her shows be cancelled, performances boycotted, books be withdrawn by the publishers, and that sponsors withdraw their support.

In this chapter, we weigh that practice against the biblical standard of bearing with one another. Are the practices completely at odds? Is there a place for Christians to boycott? How do we respond publicly when we disagree with other ideas?

How can Christians speak out with passion while still bearing with one another in love? What has been your experience of and response to cancel culture? How do you envision Jesus responding to it?

HOW DO WE RESPOND LIKE JESUS WHEN WE DISAGREE?

Lori

It's easy to understand why people are tempted to "cancel" or silence the voices of people with whom they disagree rather than follow the biblical command to bear with them. "Bearing with" doesn't mean looking the other way or ignoring destructive or unbiblical ideas.

Christians of all skin colors have certainly used the power of the boycott. People have the right to spend their money or withdraw their support as they see fit. That's freedom we should celebrate and exercise. It's important to be careful what and who we support with our approval and resources (Romans 14:22).

We should be free to speak up and act when we disagree with someone's views or find their actions inconsistent with our values. It's the scope and speed of the current desire to cancel, especially when combined with the mercurial nature of the standards, that gives me pause.

Fear may very well be one of the biggest enemies of sticking with a conversation long enough for it to become beneficial.

And if I'm honest, cancel culture scares me. Or it did, until I worked through it with God. Fear may very well be one of the biggest enemies of sticking with a conversation long enough for it to become beneficial. When I'm afraid, I react rather than bear with. I act less according to the Spirit of God and more according to my baser emotions.

But we are Jesus followers. So we are not given a spirit of fear, but of "power and love and self-control" (2 Timothy 1:7). When we are tempted to fear, if we yield to God's Spirit, we receive the courage available in Christ to confront that which fear is trying to bully us into avoiding.

As a writer, I'm no fan of censorship. I believe a society thrives when there is a free exchange of ideas and the opportunity to debate. Banning books or removing them from major retail outlets, discontinuing movies made at other points in history, or creating an atmosphere where communicators are afraid to speak anything but what is culturally acceptable at that moment, smacks of oppression to me. I certainly want new books, movies, and art created to reflect diversity, be free of stereotypes, and promote equality, but that's a path forward, not a hand that can reach back and rewrite the past.

As a student of history, it hasn't worked well for other times and nations when people were cowed or bullied into silence or pressured to only speak along "party lines." I, and many others, support a truthful retelling of the past. I love to see the lives and contributions of men and women of color rise to prominence alongside people already chronicled in our history books. It's only right to make room. It's also reasonable to teach that former leaders committed wrongs alongside the good they accomplished.

It's important to teach in context. Set people and their words into the greater story of their day. To remove men or women from the pages of history because they demonstrated racist views or practices is to deny the record of our progress as a people or as nations. It's dangerous to rewrite history with every wave of growth and every turn of culture. Doing so erases lessons we desperately need to learn.

But it's easy for me to have this view. My Irish/English ancestors had an easier entry to America than did others (although they did experience challenges). Still, since my identity as a Christian is more central to me than my whiteness, I imagine that if the local high school was named after Nero—the Roman Emperor infamous for persecuting Christians—if he was celebrated with no mention of that atrocity, it would cause me pain. I am, however, comfortable reading about the great contributions Romans made to the world—like roads that made it easier to spread the gospel—right alongside stories of how they fed Christians to the lions. The Christian worldview teaches that "all have sinned and fall short of the glory of God" (Romans 3:23). We are each capable of great achievements and terrible failings. Pretending otherwise leaves us vulnerable to ignoring our own failings.

Evil doesn't disappear just because we silence it. I'm uncomfortable with attempts to bury thoughts, words, and feelings. Forced underground where we can't expose deception to the light of truth and public scrutiny, evil thrives. John warns us that evil prefers to lurk in the darkness and resists being exposed (John 3:19–20). Bad ideas, brought to light, wither under wise scrutiny. Evil practices exposed to public awareness may still take root with great numbers of people, but knowledge of their prevalence provides the church with motivation to do the work God calls us to do and to wage resistance. We don't effectively fight oppression with greater oppression. That only causes more hatred and division. At some point, there's a backlash where both instigators and innocents become caught in the net of cultural tyranny.

In this age of instant communication, too much gets decided too quickly without taking time to gather and confirm facts. I find this a problem when there are calls to cancel an individual but also when violence hits the headlines and people draw up sides before there is time to sort through a situation. God calls his followers to be "quick to hear, slow to speak, slow to anger" (James 1:19). This is strong pushback against a culture that values rapid-fire responses, snappy answers, and quick resolutions. It is a command that too few believers exercise.

Proverbs 18:17 says, "The one who states his case first seems right, until the other comes and examines him." It's important in most circumstances to gather evidence, hear credible witnesses, and allow for rebuttal before exercising judgment. There is wisdom in due process. Of course, racism means that the process hasn't served all of us equally. With that history, I can appreciate why people of color mistrust the justice system and want to reclaim that power through social justice. But historically, most successful reforms happen with steady, well-thought-out approaches, as opposed to the high emotions and fuzzy facts rampant on social media.

Of course, there's another response to all the screaming online. Honestly, it's easy for me to sit in my living room and condemn violence that erupts from protests and what I consider an overreach of cancel culture. It's tempting to withdraw from all public conversation about headline incidents, to avoid commenting through writing or on social media out of fear of being misunderstood. It's comfortable to remain in my own bubble of like-minded people who don't believe we're part of the problem but worry that if we get too involved, we risk making things worse—especially for ourselves.

But God condemns cowardice and the inaction of knowing good and not doing it. Revelation 21:8 says, "But as for the cowardly, the faithless, the detestable, as for murderers, the sexually immoral, sorcerers, idolaters, and all liars, their portion will be in the lake that burns with fire and sulfur, which is the second death." That is not good company!

Besides not wanting to be a coward or to be shut down by a screaming culture, I also believe my silence and withdrawal does nothing to demonstrate love for those who are hurting. The people I see on my television screen—the ones burning city blocks, screaming into microphones for justice, or saying that images from the past hurt them—are people loved by Jesus Christ.

Yes, of course there are agitators among them who simply love disruption and violence. But just as I don't want people to judge me by the wolves who infiltrate the church, God compels me to be discerning, wise, and full of compassion when listening to those who cry out for change.

We can't allow the villains, agitators, and disruptors to keep us from engaging in the work of reconciliation and peace. Psalm 37:30 says, "The mouth of the righteous utters wisdom, and his tongue speaks justice." It doesn't say God's people stand silently by and do nothing.

It's also important to note that responses to trauma vary wildly. But our responses should always keep the past in mind.

I once knew a family with four children. The children had suffered from witnessing domestic violence. The father's abuse of the mother went undetected for years, so the kids were traumatized teens when the violence came to light. Two children found strength in anger, responding with swearing, rudeness, and threats. All of us ministering to them held them accountable for their actions and set boundaries around hostility, but always with calm, compassionate responses full of acceptance and grace.

A third sibling collapsed into herself. She was quiet, compliant, and anxious. Fragile and frightened by the world, it was as if she turned all the violence in on herself. The fourth sibling was angry but determined that his family's dysfunction wouldn't keep him from his life goals. He acknowledged their circumstances but channeled his pain into achievements in academics and sports.

All four siblings supported one another. They acknowledged their differences in responding to their violent history. They worried about one another and the consequences of the paths each had taken to cope. But they stood by one another. In microcosms like this family, I have seen it is possible to remain united even when individual responses vary. Evidence of trauma can emerge as violence, productivity, fearfulness, depression, apathy, empathy, greatness, rage, or a host of other manifestations. We can't control the outcry, but we can exhibit compassion in our response.

Of course, some responses to injustice are more acceptable than others, but we can't stop with just condemning the wrong. We must do the painstaking work of addressing the source of the hostility or fear and setting things right.

We must, with one voice, condemn all violence, all racism, all hatred. But we also must repent, right? Of course violence is wrong, but how many times have I heard Scriptures about how God loves justice and that if one part of the body hurts, we all do, without rising from my comfortable seat and taking action? Why does it take a dozen burning cities for me to put pen to paper or to imagine I may have a role in the healing?

As I sit spectating while people protest, riot, or weep to be heard, valued, or recognized, I wonder if I would be motivated to search my

heart before God if there were no flames. If there were no trash bar-
rels hurled through shop windows, would I be moved from comfort
to discomfort? This doesn't justify the violence, but it does highlight
my habit of insensitivity to the Holy Spirit when it's not my pain
that's at issue. It aligns me with them before God, and removes me
from the seat of judgment to join those I have judged.

I know I'm not alone in wrestling with how to respond to different
forms of public protest. Maybe, like me, you too hate to see violence
but also understand the anger that comes with prolonged injustice.
Do you wrestle with knowing how to express compassion while also
condemning violence?

For me, part of the answer lies in not wasting time imagining there
is an easy road or a single answer. Someone wisely said, "Do what you
can, not what you can't." I can't create peace in the inner cities or stop
people on social media from demanding that others be cancelled. But
I can take the fear it raises in me to God and ask for direction. I can
move out of my comfort bubble and initiate real conversations with
people who are wrestling with the pain of daily racism. I can work to
hear more than one side.

Paul demonstrated in Athens how to engage those who oppose
the truth of the gospel. The Scripture says Paul was "provoked" at
the prevalence of their idols (Acts 17:16–34). So he invested time
reasoning in the synagogue and in the marketplace. He observed
their culture and demonstrated an understanding of it. He expressed
appreciation that they acknowledged an unknown god and then
explained the truth of God in words they could understand.

We can follow Paul's example when our culture "provokes" us.
We can vary our news sources. We can choose not to rely on any one
news outlet, and ensure that we listen to newscasts that lean both
right and left. Conventional wisdom says "the truth lies somewhere
in the middle." I don't believe that. The truth lies where the truth
stands. Period. There are two sides to every story, but sometimes one
side is lying. Or one side has been influenced by trauma, agitators, or
fear. One of my regular prayers, *Father God, bring the truth into the
light*, references Luke 12:2, "Nothing is covered up that will not be

revealed, or hidden that will not be known." In watching a variety of newscasts, I hear people of all colors agree on the problem but disagree on the solution.

Personality, upbringing, faith, education, economic status, geography, culture, experience, and skin color all have an impact on our individual opinions. Trauma can also play a role in our perspectives and the actions we choose to take.

In my work I've encountered studies of the impact of generational trauma—such as the effect the Holocaust had on the great-grandchildren of survivors or the ripple effect of slavery on the current generation of blacks whose ancestors were slaves (otherwise known as ADOS—American Descendants of Slaves). I don't agree with every conclusion of how to help these generations heal, but I respect the reality of the need for healing. Just as I have for my own family, I pray warfare prayers against generational trauma and generational sin on behalf of our nation and of the church.

Violence can stem from trauma and simultaneously perpetuate trauma, so it's vital that we look for the exit ramp off the vicious cycle.

What can we do better and in more loving ways that would elevate our culture's public conversation to reach both angry, looting gangs and lone-wolf gunmen? What if part of the solution is hearing and addressing the pain of all young men and not sorting them by skin color? Is cancel culture just a form of social violence? How might a greater application of scriptural directives, demonstrated by believers, impact society for the greater good?

It's essential that we let neither complacency nor violence rule. We cannot let either cancel culture or silence dominate. There is a time to be silent, but not when injustice or hatred are in play. Justice and freedom for all people need to permeate the work of the church. Racial healing shouldn't be an elective ministry but should inform our vision in every aspect of ministry.

That's not always comfortable. It requires asking hard questions, having conversations we'd rather avoid, working more slowly than some would like, and truly listening with an eye toward seeing where we might be wrong.

When others cry out, exercise self-control and discernment before reacting. When others are angry, demonstrate patient listening, loving boundaries, and the same mercy you'd like to receive if your pain were to cause you to lash out. Believe people's stories. Don't dismiss experiences different from your own. And refuse to cave to fear. Fear divides. Love heals. It's that simple and that complex.

Saundra

My first public encounter with cancel culture occurred in 2012 when a group of individuals became upset with Chick-fil-A after their CEO, Dan Cathy, voiced his belief in marriage being between a man and a woman. The interview caused an uproar. All those who disagreed with Cathy's statement worked together in an attempt to cripple this fast-food chain via a national boycott. No one knew what the outcome would be from their efforts. Would Christians rally behind the restaurant? Or would those offended cause a significant enough income deficit to make the franchise question if they should continue to stand by their beliefs?

News stories popped up every week from "kiss-ins," where same-sex couples would show affection inside restaurants, to "drive-bys," where protesters would overwhelm the drive-through lines to order water, knowing the restaurants provided it for free. All these actions were attempting to cause Chick-fil-A to lose popularity and its place as one of the leading fast-food restaurant chains.

I remember chatting with my husband about the national boycott day. Would we go and sit in a long line for a chicken sandwich to show our support? Did it really matter? What difference would it make anyway? It's chicken, for goodness' sake.

I battled with these questions and now understand that this experience was my litmus test on cancel culture. In 2012 cancel culture had not yet been defined, but we witnessed the very public birth of it. One offended group decided they didn't like what was being said, so they decided to silence the offender.

In the case of Chick-fil-A, the offensive statement was one most Christians view as being a foundational part of the Bible. Now, the offensive comments leading to calls to cancel individuals or organizations can be due to religious views, world views, political views, racial views, or any other divisive aspect of life. Chick-fil-A may have been the first time I saw cancel culture openly discussed, but it was not the first time I had witnessed it. My first encounter with cancel culture occurred in my grade school American history class.

While I agree with Lori's statements about the value of sharing history in context and her call to make room for all voices, for a long time there was a glaring lack of people of color in history books and classes. Their stories have been canceled from history texts, erased from most classrooms, and diminished in our culture.

Before the movie *Hidden Figures*, most of the world did not know that women processed most data before computers became the norm, often black women.[1] Their role in space exploration was canceled, the focus instead being on those in more visible positions and often of the majority race and gender. What effect would this knowledge have had on STEM professions if, before 2017, women of color saw others who looked like them excelling at complex math and science? I suspect the cultural and gender landscape of electronics and technology would look very different than it currently does.

I was overjoyed when my son's 9th-grade teacher sent a letter to parents seeking permission to share the movie *Glory* with the class. This movie shares the story of the U.S. Civil War's first all-black volunteer company. As someone who grew up in the South, every history book I read only discussed white Civil War participants. It was refreshing to have a white history teacher recognize that this black representation in the war had been canceled from the history books and fight to share it with her students. Wouldn't it be amazing if all our new history textbooks rectified the omission of contributions from people of color?

Ultimately, it's good to recognize that cancel culture is not new. It's been a silent undercurrent directing perspectives and views in culture for decades.

Our current use of the term *cancel culture* focuses on the swift and vast removal of support from individuals who do not conform to our beliefs and standards of right and wrong. Lori's reference to James 1:19 is what I see as a core problem with cancel culture. Unlike God's call for his followers to be "quick to hear, slow to speak, slow to anger," we do the opposite. We are quick to hear and get offended, upset, and angry. We are even quicker to speak our minds and respond from our place of woundedness without time to process our emotional response. We are slow to listen from a place of love. We are slow to extend grace for being flawed humans. We are slow to extend the same compassion we have ourselves received during our times of failing to be Christlike.

> *Emotionally charged decision-making is dangerous. It decreases the time available for wisdom and discernment, both of which are needed to arrive at a decision that aligns with the Word of God.*

Emotionally charged decision-making is dangerous. It decreases the time available for wisdom and discernment, both of which are needed to arrive at a decision that aligns with the Word of God.

The goal is to replace silence with necessary conversations. People of color have been silenced long enough. Silence does not lead to God's justice, but neither does rash communication erupting from someone who has not engaged with the wisdom and counsel of the Holy Spirit. Even within our heavily skewed judicial system, silence has reigned for too long. We need to hear about the differences between how the judicial system prosecutes minority groups over those of the majority.

It's essential to have the freedom to share each cultural group's unique experiences within society. But it's also important to recognize the need to determine the motive behind the voices. Some voices are mocking in tone, sent to stir the pot of rage further and propel us to more racial unrest. Some voices are cautionary in tone, sent to enlighten and warn us of the direction we are heading. Both of these voices can seem militant, but the motive of one is to further tear down, and the goal of the other is to redirect toward growth. This is why we should not lump all protesters into the same category. It's not necessarily the activity. It's the motive behind the action.

Given her background in counseling, Lori's statement moved me. "Trauma can emerge as violence, productivity, fearfulness, depression, apathy, empathy, greatness, rage, or a host of other manifestations. We can't control the outcry, but we can exhibit compassion in our response."

This referenced her experience working with the family who experienced the trauma of domestic violence at home, but many have been traumatized by the things we have seen in video footage. In 2020 people from around the globe held up signs in the streets reading, "I can't breathe." The image of a knee on a man's neck provoked an outcry from those traumatized by what they had seen. Trauma emerged as empathy from those of another skin color. Trauma emerged as fearfulness from those with sons who looked like the one on the ground. Trauma emerged as violence from those angered by what they had seen. Trauma emerged as greatness from those who stepped up to champion diversity, inclusion, and equality—different responses but originating from the same trauma.

Tears slid down my face at Lori's honest admission, "How many times have I heard Scriptures about how God loves justice and that if one part of the body hurts, we all do, without rising from my comfortable seat and taking action? Why does it take a dozen burning cities for me to put pen to paper or to imagine I may have a role in the healing?"

This can be hard to swallow as a person of color, to know that some have the privilege of remaining seated, and many never move from their place of comfort unless their comfort zone is threatened. I love the vulnerability in her statements. It takes courage to share that something horrific had to occur to push you out of your apathy. It takes courage to unwrap what privilege looks like in the flesh.

Privilege is having the option not to engage because the drama does not affect your day-to-day existence. Privilege is having the ability to stay comfortably silent, because by doing so, you don't have to respond to the line in the sand. Privilege is being able to be a bystander while watching others engage in a battle to be treated fairly.

This is how we overcome a culture bent on canceling others. We respond like Christ. We allow our words to be laced with truth and grace.

I sometimes view privilege as a mindset of being seated in heavenly places with Christ, above all the trauma and drama. Then I remember Jesus, who walked the earth during a time of discrimination and dysfunction. The one who understands the hurts of being wrongly judged. The one who can identify with my pain and weaknesses. The one who wept at the tomb of his friend. The one who, even while being seated above all the pain this world offers, is interceding on our behalf. Even from his current high and holy place, God is not apathetic, and he is not silent.

This is how we overcome a culture bent on canceling others. We respond like Christ. We allow our words to be laced with truth and grace. We reply to conflict with a focus on God's agenda and not our own. We move with compassion. We seek to bind up wounds and to comfort. We lead with the Holy Spirit's guidance and pray for others, those who agree with us and those who do not. We use our voice to elevate the cause of Christ and not to tear down his body. We use our freedom to choose how to allocate our resources after thoughtful consideration and not from our momentary hurt emotions. We walk as mature sons and daughters led by the Spirit of God (Romans 8:14).

COLORFUL CONVERSATION WITH VIVIAN MABUNI

I grew up in a predominantly white environment and pushed down my ethnic heritage in order to assimilate. I feel comfortable in white spaces because of growing up in white spaces. Earlier in my ethnic journey, a white woman in authority mentioned in passing, "Oh, I don't think of you as Chinese or Asian, I just think of you as Viv." At the time, I took her comment as a compliment because it meant I fit in. Now, obviously, so many years later, I realize her response was shortsighted.

On another occasion, a white woman told a group of people, "Oh, y'all, it's because she's Oriental." My immediate, somewhat harsh response was, "That is not a very appropriate term to use. It is kind of akin to the N-word." She did not understand the derogatory nature of the term *Oriental*. Looking back, I wish I hadn't shut down the conversation so hard or quickly.

Jesus instructed people in Matthew 18:15 to first approach a person individually if they did wrong. If I could do it over again, I would have pulled her aside and said, "Hey, back when we were having lunch, you used the word *Oriental*. I just want you to know and understand that, as an Asian American, it's a hurtful term and no longer used." I think giving people the benefit of the doubt is appropriate, and when possible, also provide a little history. These kinds of conversations are complicated, individual, and should be addressed case by case.

I don't like conflict. I don't want to put anyone on the defensive and prefer not to bring uncomfortable attention to myself by addressing difficult topics. But I'm learning it really is considerate and loving to pull someone aside and correct misinformation. In today's society we are quick to cancel people and decide categorically that the person is hard-hearted or being uncivilized. Instead, as believers we are called to love people and obey Jesus's example. This heart posture helps motivate me to have hard conversations.

Discernment is necessary, in certain circumstances, to protect my heart. I might need to step back if I am worn out, extremely stressed, or there are other factors in my life that are evoking a lot of emotions.

In those times, I need to prioritize my mental health and not engage in conversation, because the rejection of me offering a piece of personal information may not be worth how much it depletes me.

One perspective that has helped me as a woman of color is understanding that each time I offer correction, instruction, and perspective, I do so as a gift to the individual or organization. A gift does not require reciprocation, and it is not a right; it is a gift. Different from teaching from a passage of Scripture, where I am objective and emotionally removed, when I open my heart and share from my lived experience as an ethnic minority in the United States of America, especially the hurtful experiences, I am opening a vulnerable place to others. When I approach sharing my ethnic journey as offering a gift, I experience more agency, and less rides on how the person responds.

VIVIAN MABUNI is a national speaker, founder and host of *Someday Is Here* podcast (for AAPI women leaders), and the author of *Open Hand Willing Heart*. Her ethnicity is Chinese American.

STEP 6: BEAR WITH ONE ANOTHER EVEN WHEN IT'S COMPLICATED.

God wouldn't have to command us to bear with one another if the instruction only applies when it is easy. It can help to spend time in God's presence, remembering all he's forgiven us and all the ways he's been willing to bear with us when we cry out or lash out at him. He is our role model.

Cultural pressures tempt us to fear, to hide, to remain in our own bubble, or to withdraw, but God tells us not to be afraid. Commit to the conversation even when it's uncomfortable, loud, angry, sorrowful, complicated, or messy. Stay in even when you get it wrong and have to ask for forgiveness. Stick with it and your faithfulness will testify to God's great love. Consider Jesus's willingness to bear with us and to leave the comfort of his throne to suffer alongside us on earth.

Scripture

Reflect on Ephesians 4:1–6. What is the attitude Paul encourages here? What does that look like in this conversation about race?

Meditate on 1 Corinthians 12:26. In what ways do we all hurt because of racism? How does violence reflect people's pain? What are ways to give ear to the pain without supporting violence?

Re-read the Sermon on the Mount. In particular, read Matthew 5:1–26, 38–48, as well as 7:1–5 and 12. How might this apply to our public expressions of anger and to our call to bear with one another in love?

Starting Places

- If you've never had the experience of being in the minority in a room full of people or in a worship service, seek out the experience and prayerfully process how you felt. If you have had that experience, consider how you would describe it to those who haven't, so they can better relate.
- Invite a friend you trust, who is a different ethnicity than you, to watch the evening news with you, then share your thoughts with one another both about the news and about how it was presented.
- Brainstorm ways to respond to people who express abhorrent or inappropriate ideas other than canceling. Make a list of ways the Bible tells us to respond to others in all circumstances. Bible Gateway (https://www.biblegateway.com/) and Crosswalk (https://www.crosswalk.com/) are online resources for searching the Bible or going deeper on specific topics.

Chapter Seven

LOVE JUSTICE

NONE OF US WANTS to be guilty of hypocrisy.

Most Christians want to be known as people who live according to what they believe. The struggle is knowing what action is the right one. What does justice look like in any given situation? Reasonable Christians sometimes disagree on what form of action is biblical. We've seen this not just in modern times, but historically.

But as we've seen, finding the right course isn't as clear as one would hope. There are no shortcuts when it comes to determining the right actions individual believers should take to promote racial healing and justice. Listening to experts in the Bible, in history, in law, and in cultural experience are part of the process. Getting informed on local situations can direct individuals and congregations in how to pray about specific action steps that may result in both positive community change and in gospel witness.

As we discuss justice and taking action, consider what action you may take in your sphere of influence, and meditate on what you believe justice looks like in your world.

WHAT DOES BIBLICAL JUSTICE LOOK LIKE IN OUR TIMES?

Saundra

Growing up, I enjoyed watching courtroom TV shows. One of my favorites was *Judge Judy*. During one episode, a man took his roommate to trial. One night the roommate had borrowed his car keys without asking first. On his drive home from running his errands, the car broke down.

The roommate tried to call the owner but was unable to reach him. So he left the vehicle abandoned on the side of the road and called a taxi to take him home. The following day, the car owner went outside to hop into his ride to go to work only to find it missing. He grabbed his phone to call the police and noticed the text messages left by his roommate the previous night.

He ran into the bedroom where his roommate was sleeping to confront him and ask where he could find his car. His roommate called a taxi to take them to the location. When they arrived, the car had been vandalized. The passenger window was broken and all valuables inside the vehicle had been removed, including the owner's wallet. Any friendship between these two ended that day. The owner demanded justice in the form of financial restitution for his lost property and for the emotional damage he endured while dealing with the theft of his credit cards.

The judge asked the roommate, "You don't feel you owe him anything?"

The roommate responded, "It's not my fault, Judge! I locked up the car that night. I did everything I could do. The car was fine when I left. I am not the one who should have to pay. The thief should be the one standing here."

At that moment, the owner started yelling about the roommate taking the car without permission. He said that had the roommate awakened him that night asking to borrow the car, he would have told him yes, but he would have taken the wallet out first. "You didn't ask! You assumed it was okay. That assumption has ruined my credit and cost me many sleepless nights." Tempers continued to flare, and voices battled for position. Then a sound pierced the courtroom as the judge's gavel slammed forcefully against the sounding block.

"That will be enough!" bellowed the judge as she turned to face the defendant. "You may not have been the person who broke the car windows or stole the property inside, but you admit to using the plaintiff's property without his permission. Your actions placed his property in a vulnerable position which led to the resulting damage. For that, you are guilty and must pay restitution."

This courtroom case is how I grew up viewing racial injustice. On August 20, 1619, twenty kidnapped individuals from the African country of Angola arrived in Jamestown, a British colony of Virginia. These twenty were a small selection from the more than three hundred fifty Africans taken from their homes. These individuals were taken without their permission. No one asked if they wanted to go work in a new country. There were no job applications on file and no agreement on the work terms. Each was forced to comply at the threat of losing their life. Almost half of those captured died aboard the slave ships during the intercontinental crossing due to unsanitary conditions.

Some historians report the slaves were initially abducted by the Portuguese, whose ship was later attacked by pirates. Those pirates were the ones who docked at Jamestown, looking to trade twenty of their prisoners in exchange for food. English colonists bought those twenty individuals, marking the beginning of two and a half centuries of slavery in North America.[1]

Some would argue the point over who did the kidnapping. Others argue over whether slavery is wrong, since indentured slavery is mentioned throughout history. But these arguments fail to focus on the fact that we are not talking about property. We are talking about people.

Property like cars, land, and other inanimate items don't have emotions and memories. They can be injured without feeling pain. They can be damaged without lasting wounds. They can be mistreated without being able to recall the abuse. Not so with the living.

Regardless of how we view history and regardless of who we choose to blame for creating the opportunity for this injustice to occur, the cry for restitution remains in those injured by the actions of others.

It hurts when I sit down with a friend of a different race and share about the history of slavery, only to have them shrug it off. Their indifference feels like a dismissal of my existence. I once asked a friend why she refused to talk about this topic with me. Her answer surprised me.

"I don't like to talk about slavery. I grew up in the South. My family history could include owning slaves at some point. To think my distant relative may have participated in lynching, raping, or selling someone in your family is a burden I can't bear."

I was not asking her to bear the burden of the sins of her family. I was not asking her to pay me back for the wrongs of a generation. I was not asking for restitution of the evils of the past. I wanted my friend to be willing to join me in processing the pain. I wanted her to join me in lamenting the injustice. I wanted her to join me in praying this prayer offered by Latasha Morrison, founder of Be the Bridge:

> Lord, we confess as a church that we have modified the meaning of the gospel to justify our lack of effort to pursue justice for the oppressed. We have altered the nature of the gospel message in order to remain focused on our personal piety at the expense of caring for the needs of others. We confess we have created a gospel that is manageable so as to avoid entering into the pain, struggle, and discomfort of bearing one another's burdens—and therefore we have failed to fulfill the law of Christ.[2]

Justice has many facets. The judicial system ruling within US courtrooms focuses on punishing those who do wrong—prosecuting those individuals and making them pay for their crimes. In contrast, the justice of God focuses on the character of God. Ecclesiastes 12:14

reminds us, "For God will bring every deed into judgment, including every hidden thing, whether it is good or evil" (NIV). But God's judgment does not stop with the acknowledgment of right and wrong. His judgment leads us to a deeper understanding of his attributes of love, grace, holiness, righteousness, mercy, and goodness.

Biblical justice includes both retribution and restoration. Timothy Keller defined biblical justice by four facets: radical generosity, universal equality, life-changing advocacy, and asymmetrical responsibility.[3]

Radical generosity pours back into lonely places. It restores faith, renews joy, and elevates humanity. It speaks peace to the weary and hope to the hopeless. It is an invitation to share what you have. It asks you to hold your possessions loosely before God. It calls you to be a good steward of the blessings in your life.

Universal equality redeems the respect that has been lost. It reconfirms every individual's worth and dignity regardless of race, ethnicity, nationality, social-economic status, gender, age, or any other societal classifications. It welcomes others into the fold with opportunities for partnership, advancement, and friendship.

Life-changing advocacy is the act of supporting, recommending, pleading in favor of, and taking up the cause of another. It is the active consideration of the needs of someone else and doing something to meet those needs. It acknowledges the reality of the unequal distribution of opportunities and resources among certain groups. It stands in the gap as a bridge for change by investing in and empowering the disadvantaged.

> *Racial justice is not for the sake of checking off a box to determine who is to blame for systemic racism, but for the sake of the people left to endure the aftermath.*

Asymmetrical responsibility has both a corporate and an individual component. Responsibility does not relate only to whether you were directly involved in an injustice but also to how you respond to it. Two questions to ask yourself are: In what ways can the church reflect biblical justice? And in what ways can I reflect biblical justice?

Racial justice is not for the sake of checking off a box to determine who is to blame for systemic racism, but for the sake of the people left to endure the aftermath. It is a process of identifying the pain inflicted and healing the wounds left by the injustice.

Lori

I spend my days (either by way of my day job in social service or through church-related ministry) listening to families in crisis. Each family member, professional, ministry employee, or state worker shares with me their perspective of the family's plight—often in angry, desperate tones, much like the plaintiff and the defendant on Judge Judy's show. Unfortunately, I don't walk around in the company of this confident judge, nor do I have the authority to insist people do what I say. Instead, it's my job (and my calling) to motivate and empower people to sort through what happened, weigh the differing opinions or advice, and develop a plan focused on moving forward to a workable resolution.

There is much about the method I use that I find useful in approaching the topic of this book. A central principle of the process is captured in the phrase, "No shame, no blame." That's a much more difficult motto to live by than you would imagine.

> *Forward progress is often unsuccessful with people who embrace their bitterness, refuse to accept responsibility for their choices, or who cherish assigning blame.*

Turns out we humans really like shaming and blaming, imagining them to be better motivators for change than they really are. Despite their ineffectiveness, we're often hard-pressed to consider other tools when processing people's pain. Usually, we just start shaming and blaming louder or more bluntly, or we invite more people to join our shame/blame fest. I can tell you from experience, though, that change can happen without shame or blame.

While my day job is secular, God has used it to dramatically demonstrate to me the hope and transformation that often lies on the other side of seriously uncomfortable, challenging conversational and emotional work. My secular work isn't openly informed by biblical principles, but I find it dovetails nicely with a biblical worldview. The process I use meets people where they are without judgment, which aligns perfectly with Romans 5:8: "while we were still sinners, Christ died for us." Then, in alignment with Haggai 1:5, I encourage people, "Consider your ways." I ask them to look at their situation and the steps that led them to their current crisis. In the next step, I ask people to set shame and blame aside to forge a path forward together, just as Philippians 3:13 does: "But one thing I do: forgetting what lies behind and straining forward to what lies ahead."

Forward progress is often unsuccessful with people who embrace their bitterness, refuse to accept responsibility for their choices, or who cherish assigning blame, which for some becomes an entrenched habit that is hard to relinquish. For those willing to set barriers to progress aside, breakthrough happens—slowly, incrementally, with occasional setbacks, but it happens. My initial task is to gather facts, understand strengths, and create a tentative path of agreement—sort of like stepping-stones of indisputable information or shared perspectives on which we can all agree and to which we can return when conflict erupts.

Sometimes families are left torn apart by abuse or domestic violence. Judges often allow children to remain with a "non-offending" parent. This non-offending parent, though they are often co-victims with their child, must now bear the responsibility of guiding their child into healing. This is hard but essential work. Having worked with many of these parents, I find this also informs my perspective on the topic of this book. While it was generations before us who engaged in slavery, it does fall to us to engage in the work of healing and forging better pathways forward, whether our ancestors engaged in the slave trade or not. It's not what's fair, it's just what is. Hard as it is, to walk away is to shirk our responsibility.

One of the toughest things I do in work or ministry is convince people to hear one another out, to enter another person's perspective, even if they don't believe they can do anything to help the other person or to change their situation. While we can't fix everything or tailor life to meet every person's desire, there's still value in hearing a person out, validating their voice, and understanding what motivates their requests and actions.

A teen boy was once asked to name his top greatest need. "I want to see my dad. It's been years since I've seen him."

His guardian stated, "I won't allow that to happen . . . There are good reasons he's not allowed to even correspond with his father."

The boy's youth pastor weighed in. "It doesn't make sense to make that a priority. It wouldn't be helpful for him to be allowed contact with his father."

When asked if he understood the concerns named by the adults, he shrugged. "Yeah, I get it. I know they're just trying to protect me. But I still want it on that list. My dad is the most important thing missing in my life."

The teen's need remained on the list with the understanding that often, the greatest needs driving our behaviors are those that are being thwarted or that cannot be easily met. Everyone agreed with the reasons that the teen couldn't have a relationship with his father, but that didn't reduce his need for his father. Leaving that at the top of his needs list served as a reminder that he was trying to manage life with a major unmet need.

His guardian said, "I don't know if I can stand seeing that and thinking about it every time I read this list."

The teen replied, "Even if it means that for that short time, I'll know I'm not feeling that pain alone?"

The unmet priority altered everyone's perspective and was a building block for moving forward. The teen felt heard and respected. He didn't get what he wanted, but the hole his father left in his life was no longer something unspoken or shameful. It was an open conversation with those who cared about him. His guardian learned to face this truth of the teen's life and not flinch. The pastor was able to do brilliant work with both of them.

When rendering justice is within our power, we must deliver it. But it often is not in our power to right a wrong that has been done to a person. We cannot meet every need. Still, that doesn't mean we get a pass on participating in the work at hand. We can demonstrate compassion and provide the smallest mercy in our willingness to hear people out, believe them, validate their pain, and walk forward together. To acknowledge that they live with an unmet longing for a justice that may not arrive until we step into eternity, where God will set all things right.

I confess, I have small faith in us as humans to administer justice. Most of my hopes for justice lie on the other side of Christ's return. And yet I know I must not shy away from the arduous effort justice entails.

But we also mustn't imagine that justice is complete healing. A victim may receive justice when their offender is sentenced to prison, yet they still may not be whole or healed. The good news is that God is present in the work of forgiveness, mercy, and the extension of grace once justice has played its part.

In Micah 6:8, God calls us to live in this manner. "He has told you, O man, what is good; and what does the Lord require of you but to do justice, and to love kindness, and to walk humbly with your God?" Some translations interpret the word for kindness as mercy. To do justice. To love mercy. To walk humbly with God. This is the drumbeat of every heart walking in step with Christ.

Having lived for many years on this side of the cross, we are tempted to forget that grace came with a price. God loves justice. Justice is receiving what we are due. Each of us, by virtue of our sin, is due a sentence of death. That is justice. When Jesus died on the cross, it didn't make our sins "okay" or "no big deal." In fact, it demonstrated that the consequence of our sin was death, but Jesus died in our place. Justice is serious and often severe business.

*God expects his people to be ready to deliver
mercy because we have received his mercy
through Christ.*

We are not owed mercy. Mercy is an unmerited gift. Mercy is extended but not demanded. Requested but not expected. But God expects his people to be ready to deliver mercy because we have received his mercy through Christ.

To walk humbly with our God is a high and hard calling, indeed. I find it in short order in my own heart and in our culture in general. One of the watchwords of my work and ministry is to enter homes and relationships with "cultural humility." To not imagine that I know how every family should function, what they should value, or how they should live based on my experience of family and life. So many of our conversations around race and ethnicity would be fuller and more effective if we entered them with humility and with compassionate curiosity about one another.

It seems to me that all of us yearn for justice, or perhaps even revenge, for our offenders and mercy for ourselves. When we are willing to flip that equation, we may see progress, even resolution, this side of glory. As Christians, with a guarantee of eternal life, we have nothing to prove and nothing to lose by taking on the work. In the church, we can agree on the goal of Micah 6:8 but still have to pray, listen, talk, disagree, confess, forgive, pray, listen, and talk again about what that looks like lived out.

The worst thing we can do is throw up our hands, fall prey to the temptation of hopelessness, and walk away from one another. And we must stop waiting for some other church, some other people, some other leaders to do this work for us. It falls to each of us, each individual and every local congregation, to do what we can and refuse to pass the situation onto the next generation without every measure of progress God will provide through our efforts.

With Saundra, I am happy to pray Latasha Morrison's wise prayer because I have also come to understand that we aren't called to solve only solvable concerns, nor are we called to only take on what we believe can be achieved in our lifetimes. We are called to love as Jesus loved, to attend to matters that matter to him, and in humility, to faithfully serve our brothers and sisters with hearts always open to reconciliation, redemption through Christ, and unchanging truth.

> *We should be fearless, because love is fearless. Love is always honest. And love goes the extra mile to make things right.*

COLORFUL CONVERSATION WITH REV. DOUG STEVENS

The deeper you go in Scripture, the more you realize that considering the rights and needs of others before you think about your own is the beginning of our understanding regarding justice. What the Bible is clear about is that we have to tell the truth. What we owe each other is clarity and honesty, including the truth of what has happened in the past. We don't really understand the present without some sense of where we came from and what has been done—both the highlights and the lowlights. We do this in our individual lives, wanting to understand our family-of-origin issues and their continuing influence. It's the same with our history as a country. We have wonderful achievements that should be celebrated, and we have terrible tragedies that we still have not yet fully owned.

For example, more than ten years ago, a formal apology was composed that related to the United States' treatment of Native Americans. It was voted upon in Congress and then filed away somewhere, never publicly declared. That's what we've done with a lot of our nation's shared issues and crises. We file them away. Some would complain, "You shouldn't bring that up because that's not what we're living now," or "It wasn't my fault." No, it wasn't my fault. It wasn't my personal responsibility. But I should have some empathy for people who have gone through it. I should see the continuing, often poorly processed effects of pain on people and on communities around all of us. It's often the elephant in the room we don't talk about. We're afraid of bringing it up, but we shouldn't be. We should be fearless, because love is fearless. Love is always honest. And love goes the extra mile to make things right.

It's so easy to begin by being defensive, because maybe the implication is that you've done something wrong. It can make you feel attacked or like you owe somebody something. That's not a great place to begin. Why don't we begin by listening to the other person's story, not presuming we know what they're going to say even before they begin to say it? Even though they may represent a certain community or a certain ethnicity, they have their own story and their own take on events. Let's start off at a personal level and ask the questions behind the questions. Questions like, "How do you really feel about that? What's been the lingering effect in your own life? What are your ideas about what can be done to make it better?"

We want to move into the future and not just dwell in the past. We begin there—but how can we make it different in the future? The church should be at the forefront of cultivating these relationships and having these conversations. Of course, there is a risk. We are going to feel foolish at times, and we will get upset by something. I mean, that happens even in our own families, for heaven's sake, so it's going to happen.

It's not just a debate about abstract issues. It's about seeing the messiness of human beings and human culture. We've all contributed to the problem in some way or another. But when people believe you're really listening because you care, they'll appreciate the effort that you're making. Let's develop some real care and concern for each other. Let's give each other grace and continue to build those relationships. Out of that, something constructive and powerful can happen. I've seen it. I've experienced it. It's beautiful.

REV. DOUG STEVENS has served as a youth minister, senior pastor, college professor, leadership coach, and as a leader in the Evangelical Covenant Church. His ethnicity is WASPish.

STEP 7: COMMIT TO ACTION.

Perhaps the first action for every Christian is to understand what the Bible teaches about justice and mercy and to ask for wisdom in applying it to the situations in our generation. Then refuse to hit the snooze button on God's call to action.

Each of us can contribute to promoting justice and mercy in our times. For some, it will mean a daily commitment to prayer. For others, maybe it's refusing to allow certain conversations to take place in our homes or places of work. Some will be in positions to advocate in the community, to write to legislators, or to donate to specific causes. For some, it will mean repentance and personal change—releasing anger, apathy, or hopelessness. For others still, it will mean preaching, teaching, or undertaking outreach with a greater cultural humility and a confidence that God is on the side of justice and wants his people there, too.

Scripture

We all know Micah 6:8: "He has told you, O man, what is good; and what does the LORD require of you but to do justice, and to love kindness, and to walk humbly with your God?" But we don't all know what it means when applied to our times. Write a statement of what you believe this means for how you should live today.

Reflect on Isaiah 1:16–17 and in 1 John 3:18 daily for one week and ask God to open your eyes to the opportunities for you to live those verses. Write the verses on index cards and place them where you will see them every morning and evening. Or read them aloud every morning and evening with others at mealtime and reflect together where they may have been applied in your day or in the headlines of the day. How does this exercise impact how you hear the news, respond to others, and view situations that arise?

Starting Places

- Read a biography of someone who experienced injustice because of their ethnicity or the color of their skin. Even better, form a book group and read one or two together, then discuss. Ask the local librarian or bookstore owner for suggestions or search online bookstores for "biographies of racial injustice." If you're a person of color, search for a biography of someone of an ethnicity different from yours.
- When you encounter churches, books, movies, television shows, or other cultural expressions that are clearly working to represent all ethnicities, write to their leaders or creators and thank them or review/recommend them in places others will see.
- Take the time to research reliable, unbiased options to receive news.

Chapter Eight

LEAVE A WORTHY LEGACY

CREATING UNITY, BRIDGING ETHNIC differences, and confronting hatred are tasks each generation must address. While styles change, technology advances, and progress is made on some fronts, sin and evil will continue to tempt and impact our children and our children's children until Jesus returns.

And so we consider what will be our legacy to pass on, like a baton in a relay race, to those who come after us. Whether we birth children, raise other people's children, or impact those younger than we are through work, worship, and words, we are all role models on some level for the next generation.

What kind of model are you to the younger people in your life in regard to ethnic conflict? What are you communicating, either actively or passively, by example to younger people in your sphere of influence? And how are we equipping those who will follow us with the tools they need to engage in both the conversation about racial healing and the work?

These are the questions we explore in this chapter and that you can consider as you read our responses.

WHAT IMPACT ARE WE HAVING ON RACIAL RELATIONSHIPS OF FUTURE GENERATIONS?

Lori

Saundra and I began this process with some obvious differences in geography and skin color but also many things in common. We're Jesus lovers. We're women. We're writers. And we're mothers trying to raise Jesus-loving, confident, compassionate children.

Mamas are fierce when it comes to our children. We can take most any hurt that happens to us, but when it happens to our babies, that's another thing entirely. I thought I had faith until I had children. Motherhood requires a whole new level of faith. I believe we can often find ways to be civil in this conversation until it touches on our children, then it requires real Jesus-power to maintain calm.

About fifteen years separate my children from Saundra's. It's a significant difference. As we began this project, my son was in his early thirties and my daughter in her late twenties—both out on their own raising families. Right now, I have three grandsons—two teens and a toddler. Saundra's sons are teenagers, still at home.

My children are older than Google, Fox News, Facebook, and Twitter. They were born into a slower news cycle, and in their formative years, while we were certainly informed about the world, we weren't as bombarded with worldwide rage and livestream fear as we are now.

I wasn't concerned that it would be a challenge to raise children to love people of all colors, because Rob and I do. Rhode Island is about 80 percent white, but in the years that my children were growing up and homeschooling, we spent many hours with people from my mother's church, which was 90 percent people of color. Due to theological differences, we were members of another church in town where the majority of congregants were white, but being a university town, that church also had a fair share of worshipers from a variety of ethnicities and nations.

It was important for me that when we discussed racism as a family, it wasn't some abstract concept. Instead, it was something that could potentially hurt people we loved. It's one thing to know there were Jim Crow laws in the South and quite another to hear Brother Roly tell stories of playing basketball for the military and being treated with greater respect overseas than in the American South.

In their elementary years, my children attended "Wednesday Night Ministry," which was an outreach to an affordable-housing neighborhood led by my mother and another woman from her church, "Aunt Jan." The ministry leaders had everything in common except their skin color. They both loved children and were devoted to God's Word. Both held the conviction that all children need to learn manners and respect.

My daughter remembers being nervous there, not because there were children of other colors, but rather because Aunt Jan would "scold a lot" when the children didn't follow directions. There were white faces among those of color in the neighborhood crowd, so Hannah didn't see it as being any different from vacation Bible school at either church. "We talked a lot about not judging people because they're poor. I thought more about what it was like being poor than being another color. But our family told stories about our grandparents growing up poor, so that never seemed like a color-specific problem."

When I asked Hannah about specific lessons, she recalled, "I don't remember overt lessons, and we had mostly white friends, but whenever we spent time with people of other colors, like at Grandma's church, they were just other people. We called them Grandma Blanche or Aunt Jan or Brother Joel, so they felt like family. I have great memories."

I was a little dismayed that she didn't remember my overt lessons but grateful for her positive memories. Hannah's middle name is Sojourner. In fourth grade, I was deeply impressed when I read Sojourner Truth's great speech "Ain't I a Woman?" That's more about me being a nerdy kid than me being anti-racist. Sojourner was a former slave and an American abolitionist who spoke boldly about women's rights in the 1800s. Her powerful, sharp use of words to illustrate her point made it a speech I never forgot. I liked the idea of naming my daughter after her and giving Hannah a built-in reminder that we're just passing through this world on our way home to God. I don't expect perfection from this fallen world and believe we need to keep our eyes on eternity, even as we work to live out Jesus's Words here on earth. I bound all that up in the name I gave my girl, inspired by a woman whose children had been ripped from her arms and sold as slaves.

Hannah's husband's family has had a long history of ministry in Haiti. Her in-laws lived there full-time once, working with young people who age out of their ministry's orphanage. Hannah and Andrew support that ministry and pray about ways to become more involved. Their hearts and home overflow with love they desire to share beyond national and ethnic borders.

Hannah grew up in a culture that surrounded her with the message that as a woman, she was powerful, strong, and had every reason to celebrate who she is. That's been a different story for my son. When Zack was only six, we ran into a group of school children on an outing in the community. One teacher sported a large button that read, "Girls Rule, Boys Drool." I was shocked. I quietly asked her what message she thought that sent the boys in her class.

"Most of them can't read yet," she stated, as if that was their fault. "And it's an important message for them to get early on in life. They've been dominating and oppressing for way too long."

I glanced sadly at the tiny world dominators she was trying to keep in place. Maybe there was a Stalin among them, but if so, he was about twenty years away from a decent mustache, never mind oppressing the confident girls who towered over him in this class.

No matter what color our young men are, there are challenges to raising them in the days of #MeToo, easy access to pornography, and the relentless allure of escape into technology. I'm sure all Jesus-loving parents try to impart to their children a love of Christ, humble self-confidence, financial responsibility, a love of hard work, the value of education, and service to others. We all pray our children are resilient in the face of inevitable pain.

There are differences, though. I never had to "have the talk" with my son regarding being pulled over by police. I never worried what people would think if he walked through a different neighborhood wearing a hoodie. My children, since birth, have seen their own skin color reflected in positive ways everywhere they turn in our culture.

I asked Zack what he remembers about race growing up in my home. "Through the teaching at church and interacting with a variety of people, you and Dad always taught us that people are about their characters, not the color of their skin. We never emphasized looks or surface judgments in our house. We focused on how people acted and the choices they made. Jess and I don't associate with people who are racist. Our apartment complex houses many ethnicities. We raise our boys to be kind to everyone and not judge based on what we see. We know a few people who sometimes go on racist rants, but they aren't Christians, and we try to minister to them and be part of their healing." I appreciated his perspective that while being racist is a big problem, the greater problem many people face is not knowing Jesus.

So even with my imperfect parenting, I believe a foundation is there, and I would probably feel optimistic about the next generation if the past few years hadn't happened. I wasn't prepared for the extreme current of anger coursing through our public debate, so I fear I haven't prepared the young people in my life adequately for that.

New challenges emerged as they entered adulthood. The cultural narrative began to shift, and now we've had a small taste of what it's like to be judged by the color of our skin. To be identified as oppressors. To be labeled racist or supremacist based solely on our ethnicity. It is a blip of a negative experience when held up against generations of people of color, I admit. But a decade in one young person's life is significant to that individual even if it's only a minor pendulum swing in the life of a culture.

My son is trying to be a decent family man, a hard worker, a compassionate, engaged citizen, but as a white male, he finds himself the villain of every modern story. This has given me greater empathy for mothers of young black men who, like Zack, are also trying to be decent family men, hard workers, compassionate, engaged citizens but who have been bombarded with negative, unfair, ugly messages about themselves from an even earlier age. And they come from generations of men battling those same damaging messages. Or for children of Asian descent who faced hurtful, misinformed messages during the COVID-19 pandemic. Or the children of Hispanic families I know who feared deportation in recent years, even though their parents were born in the United States—all from the insults of other children.

Prior to these past few years, I thought we were moving toward one another, into understanding, but sometimes now it feels as if we are creating new ways to divide rather than more avenues to unite. One mother of adopted children, all of mixed ethnicity, was shocked when she went to register her daughter (a child of a Puerto Rican mother and Native American father) for community track. There was to be a special eight weeks of track and field for children of color (funded by a grant). Her daughter was deemed "too white" for the person doing the registering. The mom was instructed that if her Cape Verdean son participated, they could "squeak" the girl in as a sibling of a child of color. The mom was confused and speechless, at a loss for how to explain this to her crying child who had now heard herself described as "too white."

Skin color doesn't make us victims or oppressors. It doesn't make us heroes or villains. Our choices do that.

We must do better at creating a culture that surrounds our children with messages that they are valued and that our skin color does not determine our place in this world. Skin color doesn't make us victims or oppressors. It doesn't make us heroes or villains. Our choices do that.

One thing my parents' generation didn't have to wrestle with was social media. This new layer of technology and social interaction, so available to my children, has led me to much prayer and consideration as to how to counsel my children regarding its use. The young white men in my life, including my son, can sometimes come across as hostile on social media. I'm always engaging them in conversation about how they're processing the current narrative. Do they understand the history behind the narrative, the context? Can they appreciate why it's so dominant? Yes and no is usually the answer I receive.

I also talk a lot about memes, tweets, and T-shirts, and the ease with which they're misunderstood, or the messages they convey being hurtful out of context. Sometimes my son gets exasperated with me. "Mom, I'm not the enemy, and I won't sit back while some people try to paint me as the bad guy just because I'm white. I'm a loving person. Being a white male doesn't make me a constant threat to all humanity."

I agree, but I also know that God's Word warns, "The anger of man does not produce the righteousness of God" (James 1:20). Anger, indignation, and self-defense usually fuel fires rather than forge understanding. And so I will always advocate for love-laden rhetoric over self-defensive logs thrown onto the fire of public discourse. I can't do the "us-and-them" mentality, and I pray every day for this young adult generation to reject that narrative as well. I insist on conversations at the ground level of anger because that is the seedbed of hatred. I want to yank those weeds the moment they emerge from the soil of my own soul or the souls of those I love.

We have a surplus of angry young men in our culture at this time—and the anger isn't limited to one skin color. (I'm sure there are angry young women, too, but they don't as frequently make headlines.) The anger erupts as violence—whether it's domestic abuse, a lone gunman shooting into crowds, or rioters setting fire and looting businesses. We miss the mark when we separate this violence into colors as if we're sorting laundry requiring different treatments. As parents, churches, and communities, we need to listen hard, speak truth into these young lives, and discern what they need to channel and process this anger into productive, effective, loving actions.

So much of this conversation is about power. Who holds the power? Who wants the power? Who is suffering from an imbalance of power? How do people obtain power, and how do they wield it when they do obtain it?

I am writing this chapter on Good Friday. I'm not sure what I believe the world can accomplish regarding relationships between people who differ, but I have great expectations of the church. As Christians, we follow Jesus who was God come in the flesh, born as an infant to a couple too poor to offer a rich man's sacrifice when he was presented at the temple. He was born into a nation oppressed by the power of Rome, a people who had suffered as slaves and found deliverance from God. The God of all power became completely vulnerable, demonstrating that he is secure in himself. We should also be completely secure in him and his promises. We don't need to grab at any power except the power of the Holy Spirit that calls us to love and serve one another. To lay down our lives for others.

My children and I have seen people of color united in worship and united in Christ. And our hope, our dream, is for that unity to spill out of the pews and into our everyday lives.

More than anything else, I want my children and grandchildren to follow Jesus. To be willing to die to themselves. To love with abandon. To serve others. To love justice. And to seek first the kingdom of God and all his righteousness. Herein lies my hope for the generations to come. Herein rests my legacy for questions of race and for all other questions that cause strife among us as people trying to walk one another home. For Christians, that home is toward Jesus and his kingdom.

I am only passing through this world. I pray I leave children who know how to love and to humbly seek Jesus, not power, knowing the freedom only he can deliver. I also pray that by teaching them God's Word and living according to what the Bible teaches, I've helped equip them for whatever their children may face.

What do you want for your children and grandchildren or for the younger believers in your congregation or community? Consider ways you can engage them in conversation about their role in creating a world that honors the variety God has created in varying ethnicities and cultures. If you're a leader in your church, consider with other leaders what opportunities you're creating for younger people to hear God's will for us, to love and serve one another, even when we're different. Seek opportunities for your family or your congregation to interact with people of other cultures or ethnicities either working, worshiping, or serving together.

Saundra

I have to admit that writing this chapter was difficult for me. Over the past month, I have been thinking about what the word *legacy* means and what it looks like in my life. As Lori mentioned, our kids are at very different stages of life. Lori's kids are now adults with their own families. They grew up during a time without mention of topics like critical race theory and cancel culture methodologies. For my teen sons, these phrases are a part of the conversations at church, at school, on their social media feeds, and around our dinner table.

When you research *legacy*, you will find it can be defined in a variety of ways. One way defines it as a noun specifying something handed down from an ancestor or predecessor. Another definition uses it as an adjective to describe outdated technology that is still functional but does not work well with the current systems. I believe both definitions apply when we look at racial legacy in our culture.

A part of my struggle with writing this chapter has been the need to move beyond the disappointment of where things currently stand regarding race relations in the United States. Proverbs 13:12 states, "hope deferred makes the heart sick." When a heart is sick, it constricts one's ability to dream. It exhausts one's ability to envision something different from what they have always known. It is a barrier to growth and pushes toward adopting legacy thinking.

Legacy thinking sounds like a good thing, but it is only good if what is being passed down from one generation to the next has no room for improvement. This is not the state we are currently in. Therefore, like with technology, our legacy thinking can hold us back from needed advancements.

Racial reconciliation and healing cannot stand on stagnant legacy thinking. It is a process of progressively maturing in our faith walk. It demands ongoing watering with the Word of God to prevent spiritual drought. It seeks to move us from glory to glory in our ability to love and lead like Christ.

The problem with legacy thinking today is that life is moving more rapidly than it did in the '60s or even the '90s. What was passed down ten or twenty years ago was not optimized, and in many cases, it has not even been an improvement. Therefore, to hold on to old ways of thinking becomes a wall to progress.

My sons enjoy spending a week each summer with their grandparents. Who would not enjoy seven days of no chores and daily meals consisting of all your favorite foods? My husband and I use these times alone to reconnect with each other, but we always make a point of spending the last day of grandparents' week with our family at my parents' home. It does not take long for these times in our childhood settings to trigger a walk down memory lane. I will see a picture taken as a child or be reminded of a past event. There is a lifetime of experiences housed on countertops and in closets. So many stories I could share with my kids, but not all of my youthful attitudes and behaviors do I want to pass down.

During one of our trips to visit family, I recall sharing with my sons how much I enjoyed a particular dessert my great-grandmother used to make. As soon as I mentioned the dessert, my dad's eyes lit up. He started sharing about how he loved visiting her because this dessert was the one she always made to welcome people. In our family, it is affectionately known as "syrup pudding." If you do a Google search for this confection, you will see a much more elaborate version of what my great-grandmother created. But what hers may have lacked in presentation, it more than made up for in love and heart.

As my dad and I reminisced about how much we enjoyed not only the dessert but also the meaning behind it, we decided to try to recreate it for my sons. The problem with this idea was that my great-grandmother did not keep recipes. Her syrup pudding was slightly different each time. She used whatever ingredients she had on hand to make the best syrup pudding possible on any given day that company unexpectedly arrived.

Armed with our memories, we set out on making our first syrup pudding from scratch. We believed it contained flour, eggs, milk, sugar, butter, and blackstrap molasses. What we didn't know was the accurate proportions of each to add to the mixture. Four puddings later, we had a spongy, cake-like delicacy that tasted about 80 percent like what we remembered. Large hunks of our concoction were placed on plates for my son and husband as we sat back to watch their reaction. One bite. Two bites. After they had eaten about a fourth of their cake, I couldn't take it anymore and asked, "So what do you think? Do you like it?"

One of my sons smiled and said, "Yes, Mama, it's good. But why didn't she put any frosting on top of it? That would have made it better."

Don't you love how kids can ask a question that you never thought of and for which you have no answer? I looked over at my dad for assistance, and he replied, "She didn't drive. She wouldn't have had time to get someone to go buy frosting before company arrived."

As good as the memory of my great-grandma's dessert was for me as a child, there was room for improvement. What she created was a starting point I could further expand as I serve my family. This made me start thinking about other traditions and memories carried down through the generations but based upon limitations of the prior generation.

When I think about the legacy I want to leave with my sons, my hope is to leave a legacy of returning to God. Malachi 3:6 reminds us that the Lord does not change. The verse goes on to state this characteristic of God as the reason the children were not consumed. Despite their disobedience and neglect of God's precepts, his unchanging love for them persisted. But rather than idealize these past generations, Malachi 3:7 is an invitation to abandon the dysfunctional legacy passed down by their fathers, "Return to me, and I will return to you, says the LORD of hosts."

The Hebrew meaning of the word *return* in this passage is one of repentance. Repentance refers to an event in which an individual attains a new understanding of their behavior and feels compelled to change that behavior and begin a new relationship with God."[1] Through the messy middle of racial reconciliation, God extends a similar invitation to us today.

The only things worth passing on to the next generation are the unchangeable truths rooted in God's Word and a desire to cultivate an intimate relationship with the Author of our faith.

Time, technology, and culture will continue to change. What I teach my boys today may be obsolete in ten years. The only things worth passing on to the next generation are the unchangeable truths rooted in God's Word and a desire to cultivate an intimate relationship with the Author of our faith.

This type of legacy is not created overnight, and it may not be something you see come to full fruition in your lifetime. When someone plants a tree, there is an understanding that the fruit produced will continue beyond that person's ability to consume it all. Similarly, a legacy should be a tree of life you leave behind that will continue to produce good fruit. This type of growth and maturity does not happen by accident. It is deliberately cultivated through years of hard work, intentional care, and dedication to the process.

My difficulty in writing this chapter stemmed from the fatigue and weariness of hope deferred, but Proverbs 13:12 provided not only the cause of my struggle but also the solution: "Hope deferred makes the heart sick, but a desire fulfilled is a tree of life."

The desire to be fulfilled is a legacy of intimacy with God. As a mother, I spend a lot of time in prayer for my family. Most of these moments of intercession have been in the secret place of my bedroom or prayer closet. It is just me and God. No one sees the tears streaming down my face. No one hears the cries escaping my heart. It is a time of intimacy, a place where I have always thought there was only enough room for two. What I am learning is the need to bring my boys into some of those times of intimacy.

They need to witness the tension between strength and vulnerability, courage and surrender, faith and fear. They need to experience the presence of God amid challenges and unexpected change. They need to know that God desires spending time with them in both the heat of the battle and the cool of the garden. They need to know there is a daily invitation before them to enter the secret place. It is an invitation to return, to repent of any shortcomings, and to redirect our attention to being led by the Word of God. Allowing my sons to witness this exchange of intimacy is part of the fulfillment of my desire to see them grow in their faith.

This type of legacy will become a tree of life providing good fruit for the generations to come. It will be free to leave behind the dysfunctions of the past to take hold of something more excellent. It will rise above offense to embrace justice. It will bear up under the weight of change as we move toward reconciliation and restoration. It will leave behind a strong foundation upon which those who follow can build.

COLORFUL CONVERSATION WITH JAMIE IVEY

My husband, Aaron, and I never talked about adoption before we got married. God just made our family this way. We were attending a church where we saw a lot of people adopting baby girls from China. We started thinking we could build our family the same way. So we walked into an adoption agency and said, "We are here."

We were naive, so naive. They need parents for black and brown boys. That was how our first son came home. Years later, I traveled to Haiti. I had never been to a third-world country. I had never seen what I saw. I didn't leave thinking I wanted to adopt, but that trip ultimately led us to our son and our daughter. And so we have been a family of four since 2010—two Haitian kids, one who is biracial, and one biological child.

Now looking back at that mom signing up to parent brown and black children, I would have told her she did not know anything. As I said, I was naive. My younger self would have said, "I am completely color-blind. I don't see color. I love all kids the same." There is a part of me that literally hurts when I say that out loud about myself. But I also really believe that everybody starts somewhere. So when I think of that mom adopting those kids, I remember the grace I need to have for people who do not yet understand the complexities of what it is like to be a minority in our country. I get a lot of pushback from the adoption community when I confess that naivety, and rightly so. But I praise God for the growth he has created in me and my husband.

When we go to Scripture, we see that God is not color-blind. He created beautiful people who look different and have different ethnicities, and he celebrated that as good. As Christians, we have to be able to say, "I see color. I love color, and color is beautiful." I would have encouraged that young mom to look at her babies who had brown skin and tell them, "I see your brown skin, and I think it is beautiful."

Recently, *The Washington Post* did an article on our family. One of my sons said to the reporter, "I could come home every day and tell you something that happened at school that made me feel uncomfortable because of my skin color." That really stung me. And I can't forget it. I remember thinking, "My kids have to deal with so much."

One time we were at an MLK parade, where attendees were saying, "I am Trayvon Martin. I am Michael Brown." My son looked at me and said, "Who is that?" I remember thinking, *I don't want to tell him who that is. Because if I tell him, then I have to acknowledge what happened. And then I have to acknowledge why that affects him. Then I have to acknowledge that that could happen to him one day because of a broken system.*

Those are hard conversations to have at home with your kids, because I have zero understanding of what they are going through. I never will understand. It is hard and it makes my heart sad. But I know from my own life that we can grow in understanding by changing the voices you are hearing. If everyone you are listening to looks like you, that's not a good trajectory for learning. Can you diversify who you follow on the internet? Can you diversify the news feeds that you read or listen to? Can you diversify the authors that you read? These things seem small, but they will make such a difference. Because all of a sudden, when news breaks, you will have the perspective of someone who is different from you.

If we really believe God's word, that we are family, then you should matter to me as much as my kids do. I should care about your opinions and your sorrow and your pain. I mourn when my kids are in pain over something that happened at school. That same empathy has to resonate within the church.

JAMIE IVEY is an author, speaker, and host of *The Happy Hour* podcast. Her ethnicity is Caucasian.

STEP 8: INVOLVE THE NEXT GENERATION.

You don't have to be raising children of your own to impact the upcoming generation. We all play a role in educating, role modeling, and mentoring those who came after us. And every age has someone younger coming up behind.

Ask God to open your eyes to the impact you can have on the people in your life who are younger than you are. Share your stories. Talk about God's Word and the struggles you've had applying it to the work of reconciliation. Ask them about the challenges they face and what Scriptures they are struggling to apply. Meet one-on-one for coffee, or make it a topic for a small group or church-school class.

Don't keep progress to yourself, but share it with the next generation. What steps can you take together?

Scripture
Reflect on Deuteronomy 6:4–7.

In what ways are you diligently teaching the children and young people in your world about loving others, serving others, living justly, renouncing hate, and loving mercy?

Read Psalm 78:4–6 every day this week. Ask God to show you the ways you can tell the next generation of his glorious deeds, and write them here.

Starting Places

- Ask the children and teens in your church what they are learning about how to love people of different colors in your congregation.
- Host a storytelling night, where older people talk about what life was like in the community when they were growing up and young people can talk about what it's like now.
- Join with youth groups of other communities for shared service projects or worship celebrations. Encourage the youth to work together to design the project or the service.

Chapter Nine

REFLECT ON THE MOST SEGREGATED HOUR

DOES OUR WORSHIP REFLECT the variety God created? Does our congregation reflect the diversity of our community? Are we being intentional about honoring the various ethnicities and cultures gathered to praise God week after week?

These are challenging questions we all must ask. The answers are often just as challenging. What if our immediate community is comprised of people who primarily share one skin color or ethnicity? What if we've gathered people of differing cultures but it's not creating the integrated fellowship we'd hoped to see?

As with every other task to which the church is called, we must rely on the Holy Spirit to guide us in this process. As we talk about worship and racial healing, consider what questions or challenges you have in this area. What progress has your congregation made, and what more needs to be done?

HOW DO WE HONOR THE VARIETY
GOD CREATED IN WORSHIP?

Saundra

In 1958 Dr. Martin Luther King famously said, "It is still appallingly true that eleven o'clock on Sunday morning, when we stand to sing 'In Christ There Is No East or West,' is the most segregated hour in Christian America"[1]

More than fifty years later, the church continues to struggle with this issue. Ninety percent of African American Christians worship in all-black churches. Ninety percent of white American Christians worship in all-white churches, reported Chris Rice, coauthor of *More Than Equals: Racial Healing for the Sake of the Gospel.* Recent statistics show only between 5 percent to 7.5 percent of churches in the United States are considered racially diverse, defined as at least 20 percent of the attendees being of a racial group different from the church's predominant racial group.[2]

There have been some changes since the '60s, but there is still considerable room for improvement. The question then is, what is hindering this process of diversification within the church? One theory is that people desire a place of reprieve—a place where they feel safe to be themselves. When there are a variety of cultures present, everyone needs to feel included. There is an extra layer of evaluation because of the desire to be culturally aware. Only when ethnic groups no longer feel compelled to abandon their entire culture on Sunday morning can a church claim to be interracial, says Theodore Brelsford, coauthor of *We Are the Church Together.*[3] Each church has a culture evident in its music, mission, sermon style, and events—but some lean more toward the predominant member group, creating an atmosphere where others feel unwelcome.

My great-grandmother was referred to as a mother of her local church. I loved going to church with her. Sunday mornings were a whirlwind of activity topped off with a beautiful church hat perched on grandma's head. I enjoyed attending our family church. It was a place of joyous praise, hopeful prayer, and community. A few times a year, we would have potluck luncheons. Every house would bring a platter of food to share. The smells of southern goodness would escape the fellowship hall to fill the sanctuary with the aroma. During one church event, an interracial couple attended—one white person in a building packed with black and brown people. As a curious teen, I couldn't help staring and observing the two-way interaction, both spoken and unspoken, between the members and the visitor.

Worship began with the choir's fast-paced song. This song had an infectious, toe-tapping drumbeat, one that always got everyone's hands clapping and members in the congregation swaying in rhythm, mimicking the moves of the soloist on the platform; but not so on this day. There was tension in the room. No words had been exchanged. No identifiable threats were present. The only change was the injection of someone of a different race.

I caught many in attendance shooting an occasional glance in the direction of the newcomer throughout service. When it was over, the couple quietly left. Not one person had spoken to them during the hour and a half together. The conversation was 100 percent nonverbal, and it communicated a lack of acceptance. Typically, members greeted newcomers with handshakes and polite conversation. Members would seek them out to make them feel welcome. Invitations would be made to have them over for a Sunday meal. There was no outward hostility, but there was a distinct lack of a welcoming presence toward this couple. It did not surprise me when the couple didn't return the following Sunday. As a teen, I didn't think much more about this encounter. Little did I know, though, that I had watched a foreshadowing of what my husband and I would experience when we moved to Alabama.

When looking at a church from the outside, all you see are the lovely brick walls and stained-glass windows. It is impossible to know what level of diversity and cultural acceptance sits on the other side. My husband did not grow up in the church. A few months after our move to Alabama for work, we wanted to meet some of the people in our community, and church seemed like an excellent place to begin connecting with others. Secretly, I also hoped it would provide an opportunity for him to accept Jesus into his life.

The first church we visited was all white. As I sat on the pew, I recalled that day in the church I grew up in when we had a visitor. No one was outwardly rude, but no one was welcoming. The nonverbal communication was deafening. The few people who sat around us asked pointed questions about where we were from, inquiring about our professions and how we came to be in the area. When my husband and I got back into the car, he said, "This is why I don't do church."

We visited numerous churches in our area during that summer, some predominantly black and others predominately white. Each left one of us feeling like an outsider. We became very aware of the struggle around the most segregated hour. I don't believe these churches wanted to hurt us, but their lack of hospitality left us feeling lonely in a new town. I do not think these churches were anti-evangelistic, but their lack of inclusivity was a barrier to outreach. As a young married couple, we needed spiritual mentoring. We needed a body of believers who could love us as individuals of different races who God had placed together in marriage. We needed a church family open to diversity, or at least willing to try.

Months went by as we spent Sunday in our home, discouraged. We continued to get invitations from people to visit their church. The churches they invited us to were some of the same ones we had already attended. It was enlightening to hear them speak about their church, compared to what we experienced at the same church. Toward the end of that summer, we decided to try one more church. Our expectations were low. Disappointment can make you enter a wilderness of hopelessness. I grew up in the church. I knew the love and support of a family church. After months of feeling unwanted, my defenses rose to protect my heart from more rejection.

Our car pulled into the parking lot of a local church with attendants directing parking. One asked us to roll down our windows and inquired, "First-time visitors? Come park up near the building." He waved us through to a line of parking spaces labeled visitors. I was not out of the passenger seat before the first "Good Morning!" greeted me. Everything about this church was different. The faces sitting on the pews were about 70 percent white, 20 percent black, and 10 percent other ethnic groups. The music selections included various styles, from hymns to contemporary worship. The expressions of worship varied from clapping and swaying with the music to standing still while reflecting on the lyrics. There was freedom to be yourself. When the service ended, the gentleman who had invited us to the church asked us to join his family for lunch. He then introduced us to the senior pastor, who told us we should come back the following week. We did return, again and again, and with each week, we met more new people.

> *This is what happens when people no longer feel their ethnic makeup or cultural background is a hindrance to relationship-building. The church grows, people are discipled, and community flourishes.*

By that fall, we had received many invitations to family barbeques and home Bible studies. We transitioned from isolation in our home to integration within the community. This is what happens when people no longer feel their ethnic makeup or cultural background is a hindrance to relationship-building. The church grows, people are discipled, and community flourishes.

This church created an atmosphere where diversity thrived. When I think about how our experience at this church was different from the prior ones, three things stood out.

First, their worship was culturally inclusive. Song selections included the gospel-filled melodies by Fred Hammond, hymns from classic red-backed hymnals, and moving lyrics by Michael W. Smith. Everyone entered a time of worship reflective of all ethnicities present. It was a celebration of cultures while praising the one who created them all.

Second, this church was very intentional in its outreach. They partnered with organizations in various ethnic communities. They encouraged their members to engage with different ethnicities through events where they worked side by side, thus preventing development of hierarchical and caste-system ideology by building relationships on common ground.

And third, they had a diverse staff that showed dedication to their desire to expand into various foreign-language ministries. Sermons were translated, and the leadership reflected the diverse church body.

> *We experienced love on a level that made the presence of God real in our life and left us undone. We wept.*

One day, as we returned from spending time at the home of one of the church members, my husband admitted, "I didn't think people like this existed." I knew what he meant. This body of believers took us in like we were a part of the family. We didn't feel like God's "stepchildren." We didn't feel like spiritual orphans looking for a place to fit in. We experienced love on a level that made the presence of God real in our life and left us undone. We wept.

My husband is what many would call a man's man. He runs 100-mile ultra-marathons, participates in triathlons, knows how to hunt and fish, and does not fear a little pain. This man wept from the power of the love of God flowing through the body of Christ. Through that congregation's love, he encountered and accepted Jesus into his life. This is the power of a diverse church. It makes everyone feel like part of God's family—loved, accepted, and wanted.

Lori

The idea of this segregated hour has always been a tricky conversation for me. It's tricky because, as Saundra has illustrated with the church in which she grew up, this segregation isn't isolated to whites choosing only to worship with whites. Everyone desires a certain comfort level for worship, and that sometimes results in worship that is organized by language, ethnicity, and/or tradition.

That worship hour (or hours, depending on your worship culture) is our weekly homecoming. The time we refuel for ministry, work, and outreach. It's the gathering, steeped in a myriad of traditions and worship expressions, that varies from denomination to denomination, from ethnicity to ethnicity, from country to country. It's clear from Revelation 7:9—"After this I looked, and behold, a great multitude that no one could number, from every nation, from all tribes and peoples and languages, standing before the throne and before the Lamb, clothed in white robes, with palm branches in their hands"—that we don't lose our distinctions when we move to life beyond the grave.

The variety God created and loves should be celebrated. No group should exclude anyone from their worship based on ethnicity, skin color, or language, although there are circumstances where congregations form based on common language or culture. The work of reconciliation is ongoing and imperfect, so we need to respect one another in this process.

Paul cautions us in Romans 14 and 15 to have patience with one another. Romans 14:13 says, "Therefore let us not pass judgment on one another any longer, but rather decide never to put a stumbling block or hindrance in the way of a brother." As the greater church embarks on the process of worship that resembles that of John's vision before the throne, it's wise for us to bear with one another in the often imperfect process. Preliminary research done by professor of sociology and researcher Korie Little Edwards suggests that multicultural congregations are often initiated and led by white leaders.

In their own churches, Little Edwards says, African Americans often dress formally and expect worship services to last about two hours on average. When they join diverse churches, they generally find the white members insisting on shorter services and favoring more casual dress. Beyond style differences, Little Edwards says, Black people in a multiracial congregation may be reluctant to push for a leadership role and feel pressure instead to settle for a visible or symbolic position, as a greeter or usher or musician.[4]

While multicultural worship is a worthy goal, it's important to respect the time, prayer, and intentionality it may require to truly create a worship experience that reflects all the ethnicities involved. My friend Brian Schrag, an ethnomusicologist, introduced me to the term "heart music," which he has now broadened to "heart arts." Brian and his wife, Barb, have, for much of their lives, worked and worshiped cross-culturally with missionaries and national Christians around the globe to help people develop worship music and arts that reflect the heart expressions and instrumentations of their culture.

This is a beautiful concept—inspired by the desire for missionaries to spread the gospel but to carefully distinguish the gospel from Western culture as much as possible. This process can be a useful guide for congregations of the same culture developing worship that reflects both traditional hymnology and the contemporary or cultural worship songs of each new generation, as well as those engaging in multicultural worship. Considering people's "heart needs" as an avenue to facilitate worship helps us appreciate people's desires to worship in their original language with traditions that resonate with their culture.

All people have preferences, but sometimes the preferences run to deeper needs that are best acknowledged and honored rather than dismissed. As we work together to design worship that honors our Father God, we must be cautious in assigning shame or judgment to sincere brothers and sisters gathered to worship with traditions that differ from ours. There will always be imperfection in what we create. But in Christ, we have every hope of bringing him glory.

That said, we would also do well to remember we have an enemy seeking to divide believers on every level, and he will exploit this issue of cultural differences whenever he has opportunity. Satan is the accuser of the brethren, and we are wise to guard against his whispering campaign that opposes our brothers and sisters. At any given time in the life of the church, we experience a variety of dynamics—new believers and old, passionate believers and stale, immature and wise; various family and ethnic cultures; different personalities, musical tastes, preaching styles, generational perspectives, worship preferences, political agendas, and life experiences. Add to that the pressure of the times, wolves disguised as sheep, and spiritual warfare, and it's a wonder that as much unified worship happens as it does during that one hour (or several)! I imagine church leaders across the land desire more diversity than is represented in their pews, but if complaints about font size and sermon length dominate, they may be hard-pressed to gain voices with greater differences.

With John's vision from Revelation of people from every tribe, language, and nation worshiping as one in our sights, we can commit to working and worshiping together on this side of glory.

It can be tempting to settle where we are and rest in the knowledge that at least the church is growing, even if we're not worshiping under the same roof. However, I believe God's heart is for us to strive for more, even knowing we won't reach perfection until we're home with Christ. With John's vision from Revelation of people from every tribe, language, and nation worshiping as one in our sights, we can commit to working and worshiping together on this side of glory.

I've been involved in worship leading and music ministry for many years. Like many of you, I've had a wide variety of worship experiences—from the comfort of my home church with traditional Baptist hymns and contemporary songs, to more charismatic fellowships, to a summer worshiping in Japan where I understood less than 5 percent of what was being said. I've worshiped in an energetic and spirited gospel church in New York City as well as a somber, serious black church just outside Philadelphia. I've worshiped with a largely Asian fellowship in Providence, and I've worshiped in Spanish at a conference in Wisconsin. I've worshiped with thousands of believers at one time at the Urbana Missions Conference, but mostly in smaller congregations in New England, where one hundred people would indicate a revival.

In all these circumstances, as well as worshiping at home with just my husband, I've asked God to show me how to worship him in all circumstances, because worship is about him first always. Most believers I meet desire to put Jesus first in worship as well. We don't imagine we'll always have ideal worship conditions this side of Jesus's return, so we look for opportunities to worship him in comfort and discomfort alike. Jesus said in John 4:23, "But the hour is coming, and is now here, when the true worshipers will worship the Father in spirit and truth, for the Father is seeking such people to worship him." Spirit and truth can be present despite circumstances that fall short of ideal.

I attended one church that I felt was the ideal fit. God's Word was central to the worship, and preaching took precedence over all other aspects of the service. The music was heartfelt, varied in style, and was moving. I was surrounded by people of every ethnicity, and there was great freedom of expression. It's exactly where I wanted to be.

The problem was that every time the minister prayed about this fellowship's "heart to reach this city," I knew I was in the wrong place. I live in a small town about thirty minutes from that city, and my heart was to reach *my* town for Jesus. After several weeks of feeling this catch in my soul every time the minister said those words, I left the church—where it felt as though the worship was specifically designed for all the boxes I wanted ticked off—and rejoined the church I attended as a child. This small church (attendance is usually under fifty) is predominantly white, reflecting the demographic of our town, but there are also worshipers here from the Philippines, Venezuela, Nigeria, and Trinidad. The style of worship is not my specific preference, but I believe it's God-honoring because the people's hearts are in it. At the end of the day, that's what matters. When the minister speaks about reaching this community, my heart is aligned with his. I have eternity to look forward to perfect worship. (My friend Brian calls that "saving some for later.") Here is where God has called me and here is where I belong.

Designing worship to ensure that everyone feels included sounds like loving our neighbors, but it's a framework that can be fraught with pitfalls. I believe the path forward to worship that pleases God is to design services with what he loves in mind. He loves for us to hear his Word, to praise him, to sing new songs, to pray, and to give. God clearly loves variety, and our worship should reflect the variety of cultures worshiping—not primarily as a form of inclusion but as a reflection back to him of what he's created. I also believe that because we are called to love our neighbor, our congregation should reflect the demographics and culture of the community we are out-reaching with the gospel. This may mean that some of us worship weekly with people who look mostly like us, share our musical pref-erences, and speak our language. We must always welcome those who join us who differ from us, but our focus is worship of him, not of ourselves.

If your community is multicultural and you can worship in a church that reflects that, praise God! If your community is primarily homogenous, it can benefit everyone to join with other congrega-tions regularly for shared worship. We don't do this to be politically correct, but because we need one another and benefit from building relationships with all parts of the body of Christ.

There's evidence for this everywhere, but a story a friend relayed to me is about a black man named Ray Sidney who has developed a powerful ministry, surprisingly, teaching gospel music in Japan (and now Finland and other countries). The Japanese deeply identified with the messages they heard in black gospel songs. This cross-cultural exchange has spread the gospel in those countries. It's a beautiful reflection of God's diversity.

Let's be curious about the worship culture of other believers. Let's seek experiences that expand and challenge our understanding of worship, always with the guardrails of worshiping in "spirit and in truth." Let us be welcoming to strangers who visit and pray that the enemy doesn't create barriers between us and them. And let us validate God's love of variety as reflected in nature and in humankind, and celebrate that as an offering to him.

COLORFUL CONVERSATION WITH DR. DERWIN GRAY

Questions I ask pastors that I'm training how to understand gospel-centered, multi-ethnic churches are: "Who is around your dinner table? What does your network of relationships look like?" Before you can build a multi-ethnic church, you must live a multi-ethnic life. Here's why. Within the context of a multi-ethnic life, there's this beautiful gift of mutuality. The best of you makes me better, and the best of me makes you better.

But oftentimes, as pastors, we are in echo chambers of sameness. And when you're in an echo chamber of sameness, you cannot have any growth. God knew exactly what he was doing by creating the incredible variety of humanity. There's only one race, the human race, but the human race is built up of a vast array of beautiful ethnicities. The image of God is not located in just one ethnicity; the image of God is located in all of God's image-bearers. That's how we grow, when we begin to see Jesus from someone else's vantage point, from someone else's cultural perspective. We need each other.

Case in point, the woman at the well is often presented as though she had a bad moral history. But the reality is that men in that culture could divorce a woman for just about anything. And because women couldn't do the things that they can do now, she was probably living with the man she was living with because she had no other means of being able to sustain herself. It was a broken culture. But what does the Messiah do? He shows up at the well and he says, "Can I have a drink?" He begins to unfold that he's the Messiah.

So think about this. Jews and Samaritans had a seven-hundred-year racial feud going. A Jewish rabbi would never go into Samaria, let alone talk to a Samaritan woman alone at a well. But who is it that Jesus shares that he's the Jewish Messiah with first? A Samaritan woman. And when you look at a Samaritan, what is a Samaritan? It is a Jew and a Gentile in one body. What's the church supposed to be? Jews and Gentiles in one body. And so the Samaritan woman is a portrait of this beautiful church. And since we're here, what is the church called? The bride of Christ.

So rather than focusing on how big our churches are and how many campuses, what I want to know is, has the gospel taken root in such a way that your members understand that Christ is our peace and the dividing wall has been broken down? He has taken the two and made them one through his body on the cross, killing hostility. That's Ephesians 2:14–16.

The gospel just does not send us to heaven when we die. The gospel is about God bringing his kingdom to Earth in us for all time, in all reality. And last I checked, the book of Revelation has not changed. Every nation, tribe, and tongue will be there. Brown skin, black skin, white skin, Native American, Asians, we will all be there in our glorified, redeemed bodies. God does not want us to be color-blind. He wants us to be color blessed.

DR. DERWIN GRAY is the lead pastor of Transformation Church (Indian Land, South Carolina) and bestselling author of *The Good Life* and *How to Heal the Racial Divide: What the Bible Says, and the First Christians Knew, About Racial Reconciliation.* His ethnicity is African American.

STEP 9: INTENTIONALLY SEEK TO WORSHIP WITH OTHER ETHNICITIES.

Consider what steps you want to take about worship. Find ways to affirm what your church community does well, and gently, without condemnation, encourage growth where it is needed. (Although, if your fellowship has intentionally excluded people of other ethnicities, confess it, repent of it, and encourage leadership to take corrective action.) Does your congregation reflect the demographics of the community? Does your worship service reflect the variety of ethnicities filling your pews?

If you live in a homogenous community and worship with those who are like you, what opportunities are there for you to build relationships with churches filled with other ethnicities? Prayerfully make a plan: Where are you now? What God-honoring goal would you like to set? What measurable steps can you take to get there? Who do you need on the team making the choices that contribute to what worship looks like in your congregation? What's your next step as an individual and as a church?

Scripture

Consider Revelation 7:9 alongside 1 Peter 2:9: "But you are a chosen race, a royal priesthood, a holy nation, a people for his own possession, that you may proclaim the excellencies of him who called you out of darkness into his marvelous light." We know from Genesis 11 that God confused the language of those building the tower of Babel, but in Christ, the languages and nations are reconciled into a chosen race.

Write a statement of what you believe God-honoring worship looks like from his perspective.

How does this "holy nation" of believers respect and reflect God's love of variety?

Starting Places

- At your church, meet with several small groups consisting of people of different ethnicities to ask how the worship might better reflect their worship culture.
- Visit several area churches with different worship styles than yours (within your denomination or those whose theology is in line with yours) to experience their worship. (Sometimes this can be done virtually, but to build relationships, it helps to attend in person.)
- Always be curious. Ask questions. Don't assume how a particular culture wants to be reflected in worship. Ask. Don't assume things about anyone's culture. Be curious. Ask.

Chapter Ten

UNITE AROUND OUR PURPOSE

THE WORK OF RACIAL reconciliation is part of a greater work that unites all of us who follow Jesus Christ. Jesus charged us to "go therefore and make disciples of all nations, baptizing them in the name of the Father and of the Son and of the Holy Spirit, teaching them to observe all that I have commanded you. And behold, I am with you always, to the end of the age" (Matthew 28:19–20).

Our central calling is to speak and live the gospel. We will do it imperfectly, and we have an enemy opposing our every move, but God doesn't need us to be perfect. God needs us to be obedient and to live by faith. Addressing conflict and tension between people of different ethnicities works toward this purpose. As the church of Jesus models love, compassion, unity of spirit, and true reconciliation, it demonstrates to those who haven't yet met Jesus the power of the gospel.

What does it look like to be witnesses for Christ in times of great racial and ethnic tension? As you read our thoughts, consider what it looks like for you and for your fellow believers in the community to which you've been called.

HOW DO WE FURTHER THE KINGDOM
IN TIMES OF CONFLICT?

Lori

How does the current state of our society impact the way we approach evangelism? What does the call to preach the good news of Christ look like in a culture fraught with racial conflict? Is our fear of differences and conflict hampering the furthering of the gospel? Are we being too careful about offending our culture, and is that getting in the way of the gospel? Or does cultural sensitivity pave the way for our testimony? What can we learn from other ethnic groups about living and preaching the gospel? And does focusing on relationships between people of different races support or distract from spreading the gospel?

Christians throughout time have the same calling to represent the gospel, but each culture and generation faces different challenges. Some witness during times of war; others, at times of peace. Some preach the gospel to homogenous cultures and others in multicultural settings. Some Christians' reach is primarily local, while others have a global witness. While the death and resurrection of Jesus is our central focus, it's not entirely separate from the work of racial healing and reconciliation, especially when that is a primary conversation of our time. We do well to remember that how we live and love others either backs up or undermines our verbal witness.

We face challenges, and we also face an enemy. The devil is prowling and persistent, determined to kill, steal, and destroy. Fortunately, his schemes can be known, and by the power of God we can avoid falling prey to them (John 10:10; 1 Peter 5:8; 2 Corinthians 2:11).

When we encounter trials, hardships, or societal problems with the potential to become all-consuming or divisive, there's value in stopping to consider whether addressing the current issue will contribute to the work of the gospel or detract from it. We can't run away from the complexity of this struggle, but the body of Christ is equipped by God with everything we need for life and godliness (2 Peter 1:3), so it's possible that we can spread the gospel *while* we are confronting and contributing to the work of justice and racial healing. We can cast aside fear and keep our eyes open for the enemy to take advantage of every melee. Then we use the spiritual "weapons" God provides—such as obeying his commands, loving others, and praying in all circumstances—to remind Satan of his defeat at the cross as we continue all the work (2 Corinthians 10:4).

Reconciliation has been part of the work since the birth of the church. In Ephesians 4:32, Paul introduces the work of reconciliation between people. But Paul is also clear that the process begins by being reconciled to Christ in 2 Corinthians 5:17–19: "Therefore, if anyone is in Christ, he is a new creation. The old has passed away; behold, the new has come. All this is from God, who through Christ reconciled us to himself and gave us the ministry of reconciliation; that is, in Christ God was reconciling the world to himself, not counting their trespasses against them, and entrusting to us the message of reconciliation." Jesus is central to this message, and reconciliation encompasses the whole person, not only skin color or ethnicity.

So we bring the message of the gospel into the fray, but we also do the hard work of cultivating and maintaining the unity that is ours in Christ Jesus as the body of Christ. To avoid discussing what divides, to ignore the pain of some, to shy away from conflict for fear of discomfort, is to deny the very power of the gospel we profess. God didn't only save us for an eternal life. He redeems us to live as citizens of his kingdom now. Courage is not an elective for the believer; it is a required course.

Clearly, Saundra and I believe the topic of ethnicity and racial reconciliation is worthy of serious conversation among believers. We've invested time, energy, and a portion of our writing lives to modeling and promoting this work. However, the passion for this is driven by our relationships with Jesus Christ and our belief in the gospel. This is central to our lives and to our ministries.

In my work, I frequently attend seminars or workshops with elements of cultural sensitivity woven into the topic. At a seminar on trauma, we were asked to engage in an icebreaking exercise regarding identity. First, we were asked to choose five identifiers for ourselves, listing them in priority according to how central they were to our primary identity. Before we introduced ourselves to the group, we were asked to eliminate the first identifier from our list and then describe ourselves without it. Afterward, we discussed what impact that had on how we felt about being introduced without that identifier.

My top identifier was not female, married, social worker, heterosexual, mother, grandmother, author, or white. It was *Christian*. This is my primary understanding of myself, and that understanding informs how I view every other way that I can identify. To be understood outside of my relationship with Jesus is to not be understood at all.

Priscilla Shirer, author, speaker, and *War Room* actress, says, "I do not describe myself as a black woman. That gives too much power to my blackness. I don't want black, my race, to be the describing adjective, the defining adjective of who I am as a woman. I'm not a 'black woman.' I am a Christian woman who happens to be black."[1] Ms. Shirer voices exactly the passion of my own heart. When I turned my life over to Jesus, every other identifier became subject to this primary one of being a new creation in Christ. It doesn't mean I'm no longer white or that Ms. Shirer isn't black. What it means is that God designed us—body, mind, and soul. Our skin color and ethnicity were his choice, and they are part of his plan for us, but they don't define us. Only God defines us.

It is in Christ that I understand my brothers and sisters of color. As a Christian, I have seen history written with faith edited out. As a Christian, I know there are places in this world where believers walk in fear of police exercising unjust authority toward them. As a Christian, I represent a God who values human life—every human life—and instructs me to do the same. As a Christian, I am to walk with God exercising justice, loving mercy, serving him by loving my neighbor. As I grow in Christ and live in obedience to his Word, I move closer to those who are different from me. The same is true of my brothers and sisters in Christ whose skin is different from mine.

We all must come to the cross. We all must lay our sins, our fears, our agendas, our very selves at the foot of that cross and surrender to Jesus, who died for us. In him, we rise. Saundra and I read the same Bible. We look forward to Christ's return together, where we will see "a great multitude . . . from every nation, tribe, people and language, standing before the throne and before the lamb" (Revelation 7:9 NIV). Both she and I must "not be conformed to this world, but be transformed by the renewal of your mind, that by testing you may discern what is the will of God, what is good and acceptable and perfect" (Romans 12:2).

I have not come to Saundra for absolution over my whiteness and she has not come to me for acknowledgment of her equality as a person. We kneel together before Jesus and receive absolution from him and understand we are equal as humans because that is his design. Together before him, we have the greatest hope of moving forward in unity.

It is not the topic of race that brought Saundra and me together—it was our love for Christ and our obedience to his Word and to his call on our lives. To me, this is key. Without the focus on God, unity actually could be detrimental.

In Genesis 11:4, we read that the peoples of the earth determined to build a great tower, known as the Tower of Babel. They said, "Come, let us build ourselves a city and a tower with its top in the heavens, and let us make a name for ourselves, lest we be dispersed over the face of the whole earth." God saw the power of their unity but knew it was unity based on arrogance and defiance, and that it would prevent them from seeing their need for him, which would ultimately lead to their destruction. So God confused their language. He wants us to be unified, but unity against God leads to our downfall.

God has provided ways to unite through him. When God sent the Holy Spirit at Pentecost (Acts 2:1–13), he caused people of every language to understand the gospel. This demonstrates that, in God, we find a unity that blesses and leads us to eternal life. Now, instead of building towers against God, he builds each of *us* into a sanctuary—a holy place—in which he dwells (Ephesians 2:22).

Doing the hard work of reconciliation builds on our unity in Christ, which only increases our effective delivery of the good news of the gospel.

The fact is that doing the hard work of reconciliation builds on our unity in Christ, which only increases our effective delivery of the good news of the gospel. Outside our churches, we preach Christ crucified. Within our congregations, we have hard conversations, work through conflict, minister to one another's pain, confess our sins, forgive, and forgive again, so that our lives testify to the power of the gospel we profess.

God takes all of us who come to Christ individually and builds us into a metaphorical building—his temple, a family, and in fact, into one body. Paul describes the church in 1 Corinthians 12 as a body where every part is needed. No part should wish to be another part, and no part can say to the other that it isn't needed. If one part hurts, every part suffers. This is a road map for working through the issue of respecting variations of skin color and ethnicity. My black sister cannot tell me she doesn't need me because I'm white. If my black brother is suffering, I hurt too. I should no more reject my white skin than my Native American sister should reject her brown skin. My Asian and Hispanic sisters should know they are vital to the health of the body of Christ, and we cannot be healthy and whole without them.

If my sister sins against me, I should respectfully explain that her sin against me has had an impact on my life and ask her to change. This should happen just between the two of us. I should be gentle and willing to listen to her response with love. She and I must be slow to speak, quick to listen, and slow to become angry. We must wrestle together with what God's Word says about justice, mercy, and the true path to freedom. It's important to love one another and to respect each other's culture, generation, and time, but our faith stands beyond and above all that.

As we take a global view of faith, we see there are biblical scholars and leaders in our country and in other nations who are not Caucasian. We should read books authored by a variety of voices, listen to their teaching, and be ready to tear from our functional theology anything that is tied specifically to our culture, all while refusing to let differences that are not central to the faith divide us.

The history of the world did not begin in the American South, and it will not end at the National Mall in Washington, DC. Our stories are not tethered to past events, nor will we, ultimately, be defined by them. We pass through history, but we originated outside of time in the mind of our Creator. And if we have found salvation in Jesus Christ, our stories extend into eternity. What we do now matters—how we live, how we treat all of our brothers and sisters, and how we apply God's Word. But nothing matters more than how we respond to the gospel of Jesus Christ, and that its impact is apparent within us and between us.

The step in this chapter is to "do the work of an evangelist at all times." We must preach the gospel with boldness and courage. But the work of an evangelist is not just the work of words but also of exercising the power of the gospel to transform lives, relationships, and entire communities. Our lives testify to the truth of our words. When brothers and sisters of all skin colors worship together, work side by side, and display a willingness to wrestle with the hard things without giving up on one another, God is glorified, and the gospel explodes from within the church walls to the streets like a beacon for all who will hear.

Saundra

The work of spreading the good news of Christ is a call upon all our lives. However, when I hear words like *preach* and *evangelism*, a part of me wonders if they refer to me. I do not consider myself a preacher or an evangelist. A part of this conflict is due to the formal office I apply to these roles within the church. As a child, my church had special revival services where a powerful evangelist would preach, and many would come forward with tears flowing down their cheeks. The evangelists were articulate communicators of the Word of God. I can hear my great-grandmother even now saying, "Oh, didn't the evangelist preach good tonight!"

Maybe you, like me, read Lori's words and had a moment where you extracted yourself from her description because you don't identify as being one who preaches boldly or preaches in any form. Or you were turned off by the term *evangelist*, with images flashing in your mind of television personalities asking you to "give until it hurts for the glory of God." You could also have your own personal views about church life and the roles within the walls of the sanctuary.

Unfortunately, many of us have experienced some form of church hurt. As with any emotional pain, there are trigger words. If you struggle to identify yourself as someone called to preach the good news or to be an evangelist, I would like to share with you a story from the Bible that expanded my view on this topic and helped me to see my place in reconciliation.

Ruth was a Gentile who lost her husband and made a choice to leave her homeland to follow her mother-in-law, Naomi, to Israel. In the telling of her life, we often focus on her devotion to her mother-in-law and how it led to her finding the man of her dreams, Boaz. This has all the makings of a great Hallmark movie, and I love a good love story, but I want to focus on an aspect of the story of Ruth that we often overlook. It is one of the best examples of racial reconciliation and the power of God that is released when we work together.

Ruth and Naomi had little in common, other than their love for one man—Naomi's deceased son. The two women were of different ethnicities, cultures, and faiths. Naomi was an Ephrathite from Bethlehem who believed in the God of Israel. Ruth was a Moabite, a despised ethnic group that the Jews viewed as an enemy. We live in a world where some ethnicities are portrayed in a similar light in the news. This divisive practice pits us at odds with each other. Even without the help of electronics, racial tension between the Israelites and Moabites existed. Despite their differences, Ruth and Naomi were able to unite over their common pain.

Lamenting together is a needed process in racial healing, and I appreciate Lori's courage in entering this process with me. If she cannot join me in grieving over the senseless loss of black lives, and if I cannot join her in grieving over the injustices against whites and other cultures, then we will never be able to find common ground on which to heal and grow.

We are all called to do our part in healing the wounds to reconcile a broken, divided, and unjust world. This was also true for Ruth and Naomi. These women faced a desperate situation with little hope in sight. Naomi encouraged Ruth to return to her family. But Ruth replied, "Don't urge me to leave you or to turn back from you. Where you go I will go, and where you stay I will stay. Your people will be my people and your God my God" (Ruth 1:16 NIV). There was something about her relationship with Naomi that allowed faith to arise in Ruth. Rather than return to what she knew, Ruth desired continuing in the mentoring she received from her mother-in-law.

What Naomi did to encourage this kind of dedication is unknown. But this we do know: Naomi wasn't a preacher. She simply lived her faith. That is what it looks like to be an evangelist and to preach the good news. It is the act of being one whose life so emanates with the light and love of God that others want to experience the same in their own life. One definition of *preaching* is to advocate earnestly. You do not have to be a preacher in a pulpit to be an advocate for Christ. You are an advocate every time you share the gospel, the good news of Jesus.

Some preach in situations where anxiety abounds, and they share the good news of One who speaks peace to the storms. Some preach on playgrounds by refusing to participate in discrimination and sharing the good news of God's love toward all. Some preach in the quiet moments with their small group of friends, around cups of coffee, as they share the good news of redemption and restoration seen in their own lives. Every mentoring moment is an opportunity to preach the good news and practice evangelism.

I am thankful my view on what it means to be an evangelist has expanded through the years. If it has been some time since you have visited the story of Ruth, take a moment to read Ruth 1:6–22. Who do you most identify with? Are you like Ruth, one who can listen and learn from someone of a different culture? Or are you like Naomi, in a position to mentor and lead others in the process of reconciliation?

A popular quote of unknown origin, although it is sometimes attributed to St. Francis of Assisi, states, "Preach the gospel at all times, and when necessary, use words." I believe the heart behind this statement is to encourage actively showing love, but I also believe words are necessary to share the gospel. Jesus did many good deeds during his ministry but in each situation, he spoke. Words and conversation are a part of the process of transforming lives. It cannot be withdrawn from the equation because of our discomfort. We need both love-focused action and words pointing back to the cross. Every voice is required in this hard conversation. Every voice is needed in the transformation and reconciliation process.

Just like our current cultural climate, the story of Ruth is pregnant with tension. One of my favorite scenes shared in the Scripture is when Ruth and Boaz first met in the grain fields. When he inquired to learn more about her from the overseer of the field, one of the first descriptions used was her ethnicity—she was a Moabite. Her outsider status followed her into the field, but Boaz had compassion toward her. In Ruth 2:8–9, Boaz said to Ruth, "My daughter, listen to me. Don't go and glean in another field and don't go away from here. Stay here with the women who work for me. Watch the field where the men are harvesting, and follow along after the women. I have told the men not to lay a hand on you. And whenever you are thirsty, go and get a drink from the water jars the men have filled" (NIV). He welcomed her through his protection and provision.

> *If we desire to nurture alliances across ethnic and cultural walls, we must begin from a place of compassion, grace, love, and justice.*

Like Boaz, we should each evaluate how we deal with the outsiders in our society and identify how to assist in the provision of others. Notice that this was not a handout, but a hand-up. Ruth still had to do the work of gleaning the fields, but the handfuls left behind on purpose allowed her to overcome her societal disadvantage. If we desire to nurture alliances across ethnic and cultural walls, we must begin from a place of compassion, grace, love, and justice.

Before Ruth found justice within her story, she endured even more prejudice when Boaz asked the closest of kin to her dead husband to act as kinsman-redeemer.[2] This role allows a relative to claim the possession of the deceased by paying the redemption price. Initially the man agreed, but then changed his mind when he learned that he would have to marry a Moabite woman. In Ruth 4:6, he replies "Then I cannot redeem it because I might endanger my own estate. You redeem it yourself. I cannot do it" (NIV). He was more concerned with how others would view the multi-ethnic relationship than in following God. In his eyes, the price for redemption was too costly. He avoided honoring his role because of his fear of being judged by his peers for associating with an outsider.

Boaz could have allowed his fear of differences and conflict to hamper the furthering of the gospel. However, he did not succumb to this fear. He assumed responsibility as the kinsman-redeemer and joyfully married Ruth. He is an example of someone whose desire to follow God is more important than any personal bias or social prejudice. An interesting twist to the story happens. Ruth and Boaz have a son, who will become the grandfather of King David and part of the genealogy of Jesus. The redeemer of the world has in his family line a woman from a culture different than his own. Ruth, an outsider, was an integral part of not only Naomi's redemption story but for all outsiders.

Before Ruth made the initial decision to follow Naomi, she had to count the cost. Choosing to embrace God's call to share the Good News also has a cost. It will cost your pride, your insecurities, your fears, and your comfort. Redemption always has a price. It takes a surrendered heart to elevate what is being redeemed above any price being paid.

The reason there is a cry for justice right now is because the church has not understood truly the concept that we're called to be ministers of justice.

COLORFUL CONVERSATION WITH KENT MATTOX

When entering into these conversations, first be authentic. Don't play into the game of politics. Start by asking real questions in your own heart, and then listen to the hearts of others. This has been a key for me.

We want to judge everybody else by their actions, but we want to be judged by our intentions. It's an opportunity to dialogue with others and ask them to help me understand from their perspective what this means to them. Find out what makes them uncomfortable inside and why. Then bring your own story to the table. Through this dialogue, I believe we can begin to create a new normal in the midst of all the tension. My conviction is that the reason there is a cry for justice right now is because the church has not understood truly the concept that we're called to be ministers of justice.

What's really helped me is putting myself in somebody else's shoes. I started by looking at our own congregation. For example, I realized that when someone of a different ethnicity comes to my church, it costs them something. I started to think about the fears they walk through when they leave their traditional worship in a black community to cross the barrier and come to worship in a predominantly white community. I'd never paused to consider that they left their familiar styles of music along with their cultural way of preaching and communicating.

Wow, what acts of courage, selflessness, and faith to be willing to lay down your preference and your cultural comfort because of a hunger to do the will of God. So that made me think, *Wait a minute. If I have people from different cultures who are so after the will of God and the purposes of God that they're willing to leave their cultural comforts and cross barriers not knowing how they are going to be received, how can I make their experience easier?* I can bring some of those cultures into this environment, even though it may not be my preference, or vice versa, so that we can do life together cross-culturally. And so I find the fears may be there, but there's such a willingness to make progress that we have to acknowledge those steps of faith.

For me, being in the majority as a white male, I had never considered what it feels like to be in a minority until my wife was robbed while we were in a different nation. Because we were a minority there, the authorities didn't even give us the time of day. No matter what had happened to us in that moment—right, wrong, or unjust—they seemed to not care and did not assist us at all. For the first time in my life, I understood what it could feel like to be a minority somewhere and have that kind of experience.

I know policemen who love God, who want to do the right thing, who love all races, and who want to be upstanding law enforcement officers. On the other hand, friends of mine who are black pastors still talk to their teenage children and explain to them, "If you are stopped, if you are ever pulled over, here's how you respond," because of the fear of what might happen.

We are dreaming about the possibility in our community of having a law enforcement and youth day where the officers come out of uniform, they play basketball with our youth, and we all cook out together. These youth will then know these men, not just as an officer, but as Mr. So and So. And the officers have a name they can attach to these young people. Whether it be white youth, black youth, or white or black officers—it's a community. And I think these types of activities and being willing to cross barriers will lead to more conversations and finding a new normal in the process.

KENT MATTOX is the founder and senior pastor of Word Alive International Outreach, a multicultural, nondenominational apostolic center and humanitarian organization based in Oxford, Alabama. His ethnicity is white.

STEP 10: DO THE WORK OF AN EVANGELIST AT ALL TIMES.

*Racial reconciliation is not an "add-on"
ministry or a calling only for urban churches
or churches of "color." It is our shared work
to cultivate and maintain the unity we have in
Jesus Christ.*

Even if we don't have the spiritual gift of evangelism, we are all called to speak the good news of the gospel to those who haven't heard. It's hard to do in these times, and it's harder if we don't see the body of Christ representing him as we should. It's important that we understand the issue of ethnic divide as a problem of disunity.

Racial reconciliation is not an "add-on" ministry or a calling only for urban churches or churches of "color." It is our shared work to cultivate and maintain the unity we have in Jesus Christ. Jesus's prayer for us, recorded in John 17:20–23, was that we would be one, even as he and his Father are one. Do the work of an evangelist by preaching the gospel and by living out the inheritance of unity that is ours in Christ.

Scripture

The early church was comprised of people from different ethnicities, walks of life, and previous faiths or philosophies. The writers of the New Testament understood the hard work of uniting in the faith, but their encouragement is not to shy away from it. This was hard work then, just as it is now. It requires attention and focus. Paul wrote to Timothy in 2 Timothy 4:5, "As for you, always be sober-minded, endure suffering, do the work of an evangelist, fulfill your ministry." What does that look like for you? What suffering do you face? What part do you play in evangelism? What do you see as your ministry focus where you are?

Next, consider Paul's words in 1 Corinthians 9:19–23:

> For though I am free from all, I have made myself a servant to all, that I might win more of them. To the Jews I became as a Jew, in order to win Jews. To those under the law I became as one under the law (though not being myself under the law) that I might win those under the law. To those outside the law I became as one outside the law (not being outside the law of God but under the law of Christ) that I might win those outside the law. To the weak I became weak, that I might win the weak. I have become all things to all

people, that by all means I might save some. I do it all for the sake of the gospel, that I may share with them in its blessings.

Paul had identifiers that were central to him before giving his life to Christ. After his conversion, he submitted all to Jesus. What impact do his words here have on your thoughts regarding the work of evangelism in our current times? What are your identifiers and how has knowing Christ prioritized or reordered them?

Starting Places

- Join with other believers of different ethnicities and do an assessment (there are many available) of your individual spiritual gifts. Discuss ways these gifts can be used to build up the church. Does it look as though the Holy Spirit distributes these gifts according to skin color?

- Consider joining with churches of other ethnicities to do an outreach event in your community. Ensure the leadership is representative of all ethnicities involved.

- Consider inviting community members to your church for a night of listening and learning for the church. Ask people to tell stories of their experiences in your community or with churches. As a church, listen to and then offer to pray with people, respond to the stories with gratitude and respect.

Chapter Eleven

USE THESE SEVEN KEYS FOR HARD CONVERSATIONS

Now that we've followed the previous steps, we're ready to employ these seven keys for hard conversations.

Braving a conversation around an area of potential conflict is daunting. But we can create an atmosphere that increases the hope of having productive dialogue by (a) acknowledging the risk of the conversation, and (b) discussing some guidelines or ground rules. Ground rules are especially useful when facilitating conversations between groups of people.

As you read the seven keys we used for our conversation, consider how you might implement them in your conversations. Are there are any that you might add?

WHAT TOOLS CAN HELP FACILITATE PRODUCTIVE CONVERSATIONS?

Lori

I was at a gathering of friends when a conversation on race suddenly took a turn and became heated.

It began innocently enough. One friend was in town visiting from a city that was making headlines for protests and riots. He shared his eyewitness experience that brought depth and texture to headlines. All agreed that it's best not to judge by what the news reports alone but to listen to those who are present for such happenings. We navigated this part of the conversation well, even though it was clear that the group of us weren't in full agreement about groups like Black Lives Matter or Antifa, and we varied in our views of the effectiveness and wisdom of protests (though everyone agreed with people's rights to do so).

The trouble began when someone mentioned reparations to descendants of African American slaves. The person introduced his commitment to this idea with these words, "Since we are guilty of perpetrating this crime against black people, and since we have benefited from racism, it's only fair that we repay what we stole." That's when the conversation took a turn.

"I'm not guilty of any such crime! My ancestors weren't even in America then. What makes me guilty?"

"Your family may have benefited, but I don't see how mine did."

"Don't you know that the GI Bill wasn't fairly distributed to black soldiers? All our families benefited from that."

"Not mine. My parents didn't get money from the GI Bill! If you benefited and you want to give money to people, that's your choice, but it's not mine. Where are you coming from saying we're all guilty?"

"Well, we just are."

"Why, because we're all white? So we're automatically guilty because of our skin color?"

Did I mention everyone at the table was white?

The conversation got even a little uglier and more uncomfortable with even couples divided between themselves about the topic of reparation, the idea of guilt by ancestry, and the inevitable awareness that not everyone at the table watched the same news channels. The conversation threatened to derail the evening until someone pushed the pause button and suggested we stop for a moment and review the things on which we all agreed.

We agreed that slavery was a crime against humanity, and that we inherited the unaddressed pain of it from generations who continued to perpetuate cultural racism. We agreed that racism exists and holds us back from fully representing Jesus. We agreed that as Christians, it is our responsibility to participate in healing and in creating real solutions, even if we don't individually believe we are guilty of racism. We agreed we all feel saddened and angry that people of color continue to experience racial comments and discriminatory situations, and that we want to be part of fixing that situation. The table was evenly divided about reparations, but we agreed that we could discuss it without accusing one another of not caring about the issue or not caring about the well-being of other ethnicities.

For a time the conflict was intense, and I worried that friendships were about to come undone, but pausing to remember our places of agreement restored calm, even if we still had areas where we disagreed. Everyone at the table shared a skin color but not the same opinion on solutions. While we were all white, we represented different economic levels, different generations, different marital statuses, political leanings, and geographies. What brought us together was our acknowledgment of the problem and our responsibility before God to be engaged in solutions.

Those were a few stressful moments over dinner with good friends. So it's realistic to anticipate that conflict might arise when we open the door to conversation with larger groups or between people with greater differences. It can help to consider boundaries and guidelines before we dive in, whether we're reaching out to one acquaintance of a different ethnicity or leading discussions with church or community members from a variety of backgrounds and leanings.

I believe most of us know it's important to get people talking about hard topics, but we hesitate. And for good reason! It's not easy to manage a hard conversation. It's even more difficult when the conversation involves a group of people where there is already conflict or passionate opinions and a multitude of challenging personalities in the mix. Still, James 4:17 warns us: "So whoever knows the right thing to do and fails to do it, for him it is sin."

And it isn't just contemporary believers who wrestle with hard conversations. In the very first days of the early church, God presented believers with an ethnic conflict to wrestle over and work through. The Israelites had long awaited their Messiah. They were God's chosen people, and they knew God would one day send them a king. Jesus is that king.

God's plan for Jesus, however, was that he would be the Messiah for both Jews and non-Jews, or Gentiles. He is the salvation for the *world*. In Acts 10, through a vision to Peter, God opened wide the door of redemption to include Gentiles. The early believers had to work through this idea, and it wasn't always a smooth or easy conversation.

The world doesn't need a church free of conflict but a church that is unafraid of working through conflict.

In Galatians 2:11–21, Paul has tough words with Peter, because Peter was treating Gentiles as outsiders. I believe it's vital that we understand that the world doesn't need a church free of conflict but a church that is unafraid of working through conflict. God gave us minds that love to explore reasoning and to solve great questions. He gave us hearts that long to express love and build community. And he designed us with different skin colors and countries of origin. He is glorified not only in the resulting unity but also in the process of laying down our lives for one another as we engage in the work of coming together.

There's no guaranteed way to keep a conversation from exploding or to ensure it produces positive outcomes, but there are strategies for increasing the likelihood that Christ will be honored and people will feel heard. By investing work to shape the conversational space before we discuss the primary hurting points, we establish an environment where success can happen.

These seven keys to a successful conversation are helpful when approaching a conversation with a close loved one, a casual acquaintance, a community member, or a group of people.

1. **Create a simple mission statement for the conversation.** Saundra and I determined we would have a transparent conversation about what it's like to be black/white in our times as a model for others. We hoped to include steps every Christian could take toward racial healing and to include the voices of people of other skin colors and ethnicities. Knowing why we're doing this was vital to keep us committed when it got hard.

   When meeting with an individual, briefly discuss what each hopes to accomplish with the conversation. When working with groups, after opening in prayer, poll the room and ask what people expect to discuss. Then summarize with a simple achievable mission statement, such as "Tonight, we will allow everyone a turn to talk about their ethnic identity and to state how they would like that reflected in our church community."

2. **Determine ground rules and enforcement strategies.** This was easier for Saundra and me than it is for large groups. We discussed that we wanted to be brutally honest, to meet regularly to discuss how we're feeling about the process, and to go wherever this discussion would lead us. We also agreed that if one of us experienced hurt from a conversation, we'd let the other know within a week. (Of course, once we had publishers and agents involved, we knew that we'd have deadlines to observe to keep us moving forward.)

   Prior to a hard conversation, lead a short discussion about ground rules that will help guide safe and orderly conversation as well as determine how those ground rules will be enforced. It can help to ask, "What guidelines will help you feel safe to have this conversation?" For example, "Only one person speaks at a time. No one talks for longer than three minutes at a time. No shouting. Everyone is actively invited to contribute." Be sure to decide how rules will be enforced and who will enforce them. A simple enforcement strategy is to tell the group they are free to raise their hand if a speaker is violating the ground rules, and that person will have an opportunity to self-correct before the facilitator steps in.

3. **Identify areas of strength and places of agreement.** For Saundra and me, this agreement was built on the foundation of our faith. We agreed that Christ is central to this conversation and that we've both experienced the most brilliant examples of racial unity within the context of worship. We also divided the work of the book based on individual strengths.

It can be beneficial and encourage more participation if the facilitator pauses the conversation occasionally to summarize what is being said (allowing for clarification) and highlight areas where individuals agree. When facilitating a group conversation, help the group identify shared strengths and areas of agreement that already exist. (If a disagreement is identified during this time, acknowledge it by writing it on a separate paper, but remain on strengths and agreements until there is a solid list.) Keep this list in front of the group. It can be useful, if decorum starts to break down, to refer to this. Identify ways the group's strengths might be used to help during disagreement. Ask for thoughts on the power of seeing all the existing places of agreement. Stop to express gratitude in prayer for this list.

4. **Normalize conflict and differences of opinion.** In our initial conversation, Saundra and I agreed that we likely would find places where we disagree. We committed to continue our conversation even when we encountered them.

With groups, it can be helpful for more sensitive hearts to be instructed that conflict and differences among Christians are to be expected and not feared. Not all differences arise out of sin, and those that do can be met with the expectation of forgiveness and grace. God loves variety, and he loves when his people do the work of reconciliation. State this at the beginning, and commit to taking brief time-outs if needed, but always return to the conversation.

5. **Identify the stakes.** As Christian writers, Saundra and I believe in creating with excellence and truth. We committed months that we knew would likely expand into years to writing and speaking on this conversation. I turned sixty as we began the serious writing of this book, so for me the stakes were high in terms of time investment. Also, as a white person entering this conversation, I had my own fears about exposing my thoughts to the world. What if I say something wrong? What if some of my ideas actually *are* racist, and I've been blind to that fact?

   What if I get cancelled? The personal stakes were daunting, but I felt God call me to set aside my discomfort and engage in this work out of love for him and for others.

   There might not be high stakes in a discussion about paint color for the nursery, but discussions of worship style, racism, diversity, inclusion, or leadership may impact the group, the church, and even the community. That impact could be positive or negative, depending on the outcome of the conversation. Stating the stakes up front helps people respect that the words spoken in the room carry weight beyond the room.

6. **Encourage transparency and participation.** I don't know about Saundra, but it was tempting for me to pull back on transparency. There wasn't much room for that since we shared our rough draft writing with one another. For a writer, that's really going out on a limb. Most people don't read what I write until I've really honed and edited it.

   Also daunting is that we're not having this conversation alone with one another but in front of all of you too. But I believe in being vulnerable. I believe in letting God defend me and not relying on self-defense. I want to grow. If I have areas of growth that emerge in this process, that contributes to the humility God desires.

   It's frustrating to reach the end of a group's hard conversation and hear people mutter that they didn't really agree but didn't speak up. One method to encourage participation is to use anonymous polling with the results read aloud. This can be a good barometer of true agreement. It helps people see they're not alone (or that they are!). Verbal polling can also be helpful. Warn people a poll is coming: "Just a heads-up that after Tom speaks, I'm going to poll to see where everyone stands on this topic, beginning with Lashonda."

7. **Determine a shared summary of the discussion at the end.** Of course, the shared summary of Saundra and my conversation is this book.

   When having an individual or group conversation, it's worth saving ten to fifteen minutes at the end to summarize what was discussed and to agree what people will share about what occurred as well as next steps. Revisit strengths and agreements before prayer.

The key to effective hard conversations is knowing it may take more than one conversation to achieve progress. People must feel safe to come back to the table. These seven guidelines will facilitate that in most situations.

When things go awry, as they sometimes will like in the story at the opening of this chapter, feel free to pause a conversation. Here are some questions that can help you do that: "Can we take a break?" "Could anyone else use a breather?" "How about we pause for a moment and assess where we are?" "Can we revisit the things on which we agree before continuing to discuss our area of disagreement?"

While it can help to pray in these breather moments, use caution about spoken prayers immediately following heated discussion. Sometimes people fall prey to the temptation to keep arguing their point in the guise of prayer. Some ways to manage this are (a) call for silent prayer, (b) have written prayers available for use in those moments, or (c) predesignate a person known for their maturity in Christ and trusted by all parties to pray into those moments or lead in prayer. If a church or community group will be engaging in a hard conversation on this topic, request that a small group of praying believers spend the duration of the conversation interceding in prayer and praying against the enemy—have them in an adjoining room or off to the side.

Try not to put too much pressure on any one hard conversation. Schedule ample time for disagreement and then reconciliation to occur. If conflict breaks out, scrap the remaining agenda to allow time to reach some resolution before everyone disperses. Reasonable Christians may disagree, but we can do it with grace, kindness, and with affirmations of love for one another. Make Ephesians 4:26 one of your ground rules and commit to working through anger before parting. "Be angry and do not sin; do not let the sun go down on your anger." You don't need to work through every conflict, but resolve the heat of it before leaving.

We have been given, in Christ, the ministry of reconciliation (2 Corinthians 5:18). He has equipped us with everything we need for life and godliness (2 Peter 1:3). And so we can have every confidence that he is active in this work, but it is work. Let's work with the hope of Christ in our hearts. Work with our eyes on our eternal home. Work with the cross of Christ central to all involved, celebrating his resurrection and triumph over death by not giving in to despair. He is worthy of all our efforts and sacrifices. He is worthy of every moment we spend claiming his kingdom come in relationships, in the church, and in our communities by inhabiting the unity we have in Christ and letting nothing disrupt it—not hatred, not apathy, and certainly not fear.

Saundra

I am someone who does not believe God and science are at war with each other. I see God in both the natural and the supernatural. Both are needed in this process of racial healing. In the early planning stages, Lori and I had many conversations about this book project, much of which she has already shared with you in this chapter. One of the conversations we had in the proposal process was on how to empower readers to take the next step. It is our desire to see each of you having more of these types of conversations within your sphere of influence.

As I reached out to the many voices contributing to this book, I noticed a consistent comment, "I'm not sure I'm ready to have this conversation with others." The interesting thing is, I wasn't reaching out to people in obscurity who are unfamiliar with sharing their thoughts. I was reaching out to people with huge speaking ministries. Many of them have published books and have active blog followings. Most are leading in some way within their community. If *they* do not feel equipped to have this conversation, how many others feel ill-prepared?

During the past months of writing, I sought God's heart in this question of how best to help others feel conversation-ready. I spend much of my week speaking within organizations and companies on topics related to productivity, employee engagement, and employee wellness. This led me to pursue and obtain my certificate in Diversity, Equity, and Inclusion in the Workplace. Studying for this certification helped me to better understand the entry points to hard conversations.

Conversation Readiness Assessment

From this training, I have developed an assessment to help you determine your level of conversation readiness. Are you ready to listen, ready to learn, or ready to lead?

Ready to Listen

If you are new to having conversations on race and ethnicity or if your prior attempts at having these conversations have ended in heated situations like the one Lori described, you will want to begin with listening. The *Ready to Listen* stage is the starting point for any conversations on race. It doesn't require any prior knowledge on how to successfully do it, nor does it require that you understand another's point or agree with anyone's statements. It only requires a willingness to be present and open. If you can sit in the room where others are sharing, you are being a part of the conversation.

Long before our mouths spew words, our spirit needs the deep cleansing of reflection, repentance, and renewal.

Not everyone is ready to verbalize what they are experiencing without it coming across as being offensive or defensive. A period of time is needed for the heart to be searched and areas to be revealed for the Holy Spirit to touch. Long before our mouths spew words, our spirit needs the deep cleansing of reflection, repentance, and renewal. Only then can we emerge from the wilderness with the power to speak life, truth, and love.

If, like Lori and me, the thought of having a conversation with someone of another race scares you, I encourage you to commit not to talking but to making yourself available to be in the room. Seek opportunities for increased contact with those of different ethnicities. Proximity is a precursor to communication. Presence is in itself communication. Showing up is communication.

Who is in the room at times speaks louder than the words spoken. When a group asks me to speak and shares their commitment to diversity, I often investigate to see who is sitting on their board. It communicates volumes when all the faces within their leadership look alike, regardless of what their lips may be saying. Even the most introverted person can start at the *Ready to Listen* stage of the conversation. You are more ready than you know.

If what Lori and I have shared has stirred up awareness within you and has increased your concern for others, take the next step into cultivating your own healing conversations by making yourself available to listen. This does not mean you have to actively seek out a racial diversity group or go on the hunt to find a person of a different race to connect with. Rather, be on the lookout for organic opportunities within your day and don't avoid these moments because of fear or a lack of comfort in entering into these times of conversation. Instead, if the opportunity arises, embrace it.

Ready to Learn

Listening often helps you notice those times when you make stereotypes and helps you recognize your own areas of bias. The even better news is that being open to listening positions you to learn ways to reduce and eliminate these patterns of behavior. As you gain understanding about what topics cause you to feel offended, upset, hurt, or angry, you are more prepared to reflect before speaking, leading to more healthy conversations. During the *Ready to Learn* stage, you become more culturally aware. You start to look for ways to invite diversity into your life and include people from different ethnicities in your environment. You are open to learning new patterns of interacting with others and want to grow in the art of having hard conversations.

As you see stereotypical portrayals within the media or catch yourself making a stereotypical judgment, you will learn how to replace feelings of guilt and condemnation with grace toward yourself as you grow and learn. This allows you to label stereotypical thoughts accurately without allowing the thought to lead you to a place of toxicity and negativity toward yourself or your ethnic group. Reflect on why the thought occurred and how it can be prevented next time. Use these opportunities to develop new non-stereotypical responses to situations as you unlearn prior prejudices.

Ready to Lead

Those who are ready to lead are aware of cultural pain points, moved by their concern into action, and have invested time into learning and seeking God's heart on the matter. They are comfortable discussing difficult topics and can do so with grace and love. Those leaders are ready to facilitate conversations and can guide group members in seeing the common in-groups they can identify with while still honoring each member's uniqueness and cultural identity. There is a responsibility that comes with being one who is ready to lead. You must also continue to be one who is ready to listen and to learn. These three stages are not isolated steps but are a continuum through which ongoing growth occurs.

I echo Lori in stating that I believe it is vital we understand that the world doesn't need a church free of conflict but a church that is unafraid of working through conflict. It is our prayer that this Conversation Readiness Assessment will be a tool in the hands of God to break through the walls of fear and the gates of discomfort preventing many from entering these hard conversations. You are more ready than you know. Begin where you are and let God lead you into the divinely appointed healing conversations that He has awaiting you.

COLORFUL CONVERSATION WITH GLYNNIS WHITWER

In 2005 we brought two girls from Africa into our home to become part of our family. We always knew we were going to adopt. But international adoption wasn't anywhere on the radar until God just put it on my radar in a way that I couldn't deny that it was him.

Initially I wanted to help my daughters see that they weren't different from anybody else. As they grew up, I think they were just too kind to say, "Mommy, you really messed up on this. You should have introduced us to more black women. You should have helped us understand that there was a difference." When my oldest daughter would tell me that people were looking at her, I minimized her concern. I realize now that that wasn't the right thing to do. I needed to acknowledge the difference. She needed to hear me understand. I missed a big part of being able to have that conversation with my girls and give that gift to them.

All these feelings were simmering, but God really got ahold of my heart a few years later while doing a group study of the book *What Lies Between Us*, by Lucretia Berry. That book was hard. Oh my, it was so hard. There were so many times when I wanted to stop reading the book and say, "I'm so offended by this." How can you tell me that being color-blind isn't right? I always thought that if we can just ignore color, everything's going to be great. But I started to realize that there's this whole other people-of-color experience that I was denying.

One thing I have learned is that it's hard to dive into some of these deeper topics without wading into easier topics first. I would suggest starting the conversation in areas with some common ground, and then grow into harder ones. As soon as somebody puts their walls up, you're done.

Another big key that has helped me understand and keep moving forward in these conversations is to be willing to listen and accept that somebody had a different experience than I did. And their experience was valid and true, even though I didn't experience it.

God has continued breaking things inside of me. Breaking patterns of thought and long-held beliefs, one after another. I continued learning by reading the book *Be the Bridge* by Latasha Morrison.

While I read Morrison's words, I felt the Lord speak to my heart, "If you have a place of influence or if I have given you any open door, open that door for somebody who doesn't have access to that door." God showed me there's a perspective that needs to be represented. And in my ministry position, I have an ability to bring a different perspective and to create open doors for people who might not otherwise have them.

I feel like I've just scratched the surface of understanding the issues that divide us in this area. But I'm committed to learn, hopefully growing in understanding and wisdom and becoming the person God always wanted me to be.

It isn't always an easy or comfortable place to be, but it is a place where I continue to learn and offer what small pieces I can.

GLYNNIS WHITWER is the Executive Director of Communications at Proverbs 31 Ministries. Her ethnicity is white.

STEP 11: DETERMINE TO HAVE ONE CONVERSATION ABOUT RACE IN THE NEXT THIRTY DAYS.

What's your next step? Moving forward beyond reading this book will be scarier for some than for others, but that's what it's all about. So set aside fear. Renounce apathy. Forge ahead by making a plan to have one conversation about race within the next thirty days. Will it be with your family? A neighbor? A friend from church or a fellow worshiper you don't know well? A coworker? A person from a church with a congregation that is largely white or largely black or largely Asian/Hispanic/Hmong/Filipino/Native American?

This can be daunting, but in some ways it's very simple. Find at least one other person and begin a conversation. Listen. Speak truth. Open your heart to learn. Give God room to work, and you will be surprised at the adventure that awaits!

Scripture
Reflect on the challenge of James's words in James 1:23–27. Too many of us of every color read God's Word, say "Amen," then walk away unchanged. We must put feet to our faith and apply his Word to the everyday actions of our lives—lived out at kitchen tables, corner booths, coffee shops, and conference rooms. Now is the time for every believer to commit to demonstrating Jesus's love and truth.

In what ways has God been speaking to you through this book?

What would it look like for you to obey God's Word today?

Starting places
- It can help to work through this process with a friend, spouse, or ministry colleague. Meet together, agree to support one another, and choose a place to begin.
- Church leaders would be wise to begin this process with the leadership team or a specially appointed small group representing various ethnicities in the congregation.
- Take the Conversation Readiness Assessment. This will help determine your next steps.

Chapter Twelve

HOPE FOR CHANGE

EVEN A LIGHT OBJECT feels heavy when we have to hold it up for a long time. So it is with hope.

It's challenging to hold on to hope in the face of centuries of conflict and setbacks. We have both wrestled with discouragement around the work of healing racial and ethnic tensions. But as believers, we place our hope not in programs or processes or people but in the power of Jesus Christ.

Paul says in Philippians 3:13–14, "But one thing I do: forgetting what lies behind and straining forward to what lies ahead, I press on toward the goal for the prize of the upward call of God in Christ Jesus." We find these words motivating in our conversation. We know mistakes have been made in this work, but we also recognize that many have set their hearts to building bridges and creating unity. We reject hopelessness because our hope is in Christ, and so we continue the work.

Join us, won't you, in determining to resist the temptation to abandon hope? Instead, remember that our God is in the work, so we have every reason to hope.

WHERE DO WE ANCHOR OUR HOPE
FOR LASTING CHANGE?

Saundra

On May 14, 1961, a group of thirteen individuals traveled by bus into Anniston, Alabama. This group consisted of six black and seven white individuals who did not believe the Supreme Court's judgment to segregate interstate transportation was constitutional. This group became known as the Freedom Riders. They set out to travel from Washington, DC, throughout the segregated South visiting these bus terminals.

After many days of travel and confrontations along the way, they were not prepared for the more than two hundred enraged Alabamians awaiting them at the Anniston bus terminal. The bus driver saw the crowd and made a wise decision to drive past the terminal, only to have the angry mob jump into their cars to follow. The tires on the bus were blown out, and a bomb was thrown inside of it. Miraculously, the Freedom Riders escaped the bus as it burst into flames, only to run into the metal-pipe-swinging arms of the waiting mob.

The next day, images of the burning Greyhound bus and the bloodied bodies of the riders appeared on the front pages of newspapers throughout the country. The Freedom Riders' cause and the state of race relations in the United States became international news, as many stared in horror at the telling photographs.[1]

I've spent the past twenty years working less than half a mile from the bus station where the two hundred stood waiting in ambush. The station is no longer operational, but the Freedom Riders National Monument now stands in the spot as a reminder of the tragedy. Six miles away stands an Alabama Historical Marker identifying the site where the bus burned.

In 2018 I discovered that God could do amazing things with six miles and a leader who refuses to let you stay in your comfort zone.

Active listening is an affirming and loving posture. It conveys a desire to understand another and is an integral part of being a good conversationalist.

As with any process of growth, there are stages of maturation. When you take your first uneasy steps into healing conversations, you may find you don't have much to say but are open to listening to different perspectives. Active listening is an affirming and loving posture. It conveys a desire to understand another and is an integral part of being a good conversationalist.

The growth continues as you learn how to combine listening with sharing your perspective. This requires a level of maturity that is patient, kind, and actively loving. 1 Corinthians 13:4–7 shares this type of maturity in love that "does not envy, it does not boast, it is not proud. It does not dishonor others, it is not self-seeking, it is not easily angered, it keeps no record of wrongs. [It] does not delight in evil but rejoices with the truth. It always protects, always trusts, always hopes, always perseveres" (NIV). It is in this learning stage where we learn how to show love.

Once you have learned how to navigate hard cultural conversations in your spheres of influence, there will be opportunities to lead others into conversations. This is how I came to know Dr. Jaqueline Paddio. She was a lighthouse of a woman, illuminating God's spirit and abundant life. She was the type of woman you would not be able to overlook in a crowd. She radiated inner confidence that testified of a solid understanding of who she was in Christ. She exuded a combination of peace and power that arrested me during a casual Sunday morning when she announced to me, "I've been asking God to show me teachers he is raising up in our church, and he showed me you."

For the next year, she took me under her wing like a mother hen and pushed me out of my comfort zone. She opened up doors of opportunity for me to teach at our church. I spent months with those new in their faith, sharing the good news that those who the Son sets free are free indeed. Free from condemnation, fear, worry, anxiety, addiction, and anything else attempting to make one feel disqualified from the grace of God. When I left teaching sessions feeling like I'd done a horrible job, she encouraged me. And when I interjected too much of me and not enough of God, she corrected me. She was eager to cover me in prayer and even more keen on showing me how to pray the armor of God over myself as I went out to speak and minister to others.

She was never one to shy away from big obstacles. She believed all things were possible with her big God, and in 2018 she set out to do the impossible. She felt impressed by God to bring healing to the pain left in our community following the killing of the Freedom Riders. Dr. Paddio planned a community bus ride and march focused on reconciling, restoring, and healing relationships in the area. This was not just a church-wide event for our body of believers. No, her vision was much more extensive. She invited every church in and around Anniston to retrace the Freedom Riders' original route and conclude with a one-mile march along the street where the bus was bombed. Baptist, Methodist, Pentecostal, Catholics, and other denominations were all invited to #GetOnTheBus. Black, white, Native American, Asian, Hispanic, and other cultures were all invited to #GetOnTheBus.

The goal was not to stir up old bad feelings or raise awareness of what had happened years ago. The goal was to heal a wound that was still festering in our community and dividing our churches. In the weeks leading up to the event, we posted flyers all over town and reached out to those in our sphere of influence. No one knew what the outcome would be, but we were all ready to see a change in the dynamics of our local community.

My family arrived at the church parking lot early on the morning of May 5, 2018. We didn't know what to expect. Would this be a peaceful event, or would it disturb a racial hornet's nest? Both of our preteen boys were by our side as we climbed on board our bus. There were rows and rows of buses, each filled with a myriad of ethnicities, church denominations, income brackets, and educational backgrounds. Before the first key turned in the ignition, prayer was released over our day from a diverse group of pastors and leaders. Then our bus set out on its route to the first monument with our guide sharing what happened back in 1961.

It was a somber moment as we pulled into the bus terminal. We filed off in silence in remembrance of the lives lost, both black and white. Government officials joined us and shared the significance of the moment before we reboarded the bus to head the remaining six miles to the site of the bombing and beatings. During those six miles, people entered into long overdue conversations. Some listened and, for the first time, acknowledged the pain of another. Some learned things about history that they didn't know existed and began to process their feelings with other believers. Each person entered into the conversation at their current level of comfort, but we were all engaged in the conversation.

> *All around me, hands of different colors joined, and a song of praise was lifted. . . . and I saw Jesus in it all.*

The final mile consisted of a march. One by one, each bus stopped to let out its riders. Some held signs with words painted on them. Love. Unity. Brotherhood. Community. Toward the front of the line, I spotted Dr. Paddio with a bullhorn, shouting these same words into the atmosphere. All around me, hands of different colors joined, and a song of praise was lifted. That same spirit of praise was taken back to the sanctuary, where my community entered into a moment of heaven on earth for the next few hours. Native Americans were sharing their cultural songs to God, followed by predominately black churches bringing their gospel rhythms into the mix, and southern gospel harmonica medleys. It was a celebration of peace. It was a glimpse of the power of conversation to lead us back to a place of fellowship. It was a laying aside of the weight that so easily tries to beset us, and I saw Jesus in it all.

It wasn't long after that event that Dr. Jaqueline Paddio went to be with the Lord. Her work leading our community into reconciliation was done, but the work of healing had just begun. Since then there has been a statewide healing and restoration project between the black church, white church, and multicultural denominations. In 2020 All In Alabama was launched by Pastor Kent Mattox with a culturally diverse group of believers visiting all sixty-seven counties in Alabama. They visited government offices in each area and prayed with officials for discernment and racial reconciliation across the state. They lamented the many deaths that occurred against blacks and other people of color. Dirt was collected from every county to remember those who had been lynched, and a memorial was erected to honor those who lost their lives because of their ethnicity. These All In Alabama gatherings created an opportunity for a multicultural group of pastors to break down the walls in Alabama to find the common ground of the cross.

Their collective effort not only influenced the church but also the government, communities, schools, and the family unit. Dr. Paddio's leadership sparked a wave of healing conversation that led to state officials inviting God into their hearts and their decision-making processes. It led to an increase in volunteerism in community projects affecting people of different ethnicities. It led to an increase in diversity and inclusion within the local churches. It encouraged many to step out of their comfort zone, and it awakened hope in the power of the church.

We are not all leaders like Dr. Paddio, but we can have a conversation with one person who does not look like us. This is where it all started during that six-mile bus drive, with multiple one-on-one conversations. Those colorful connections made room in hearts for God to do the work of healing and reconciliation. Each conversation provided an opportunity to listen, learn, and love.

Lori

We are all made in the image of God. And as Christians, we are ambassadors of Christ. Through every believer, God makes his appeal to a waiting world (2 Corinthians 5:20). Saundra and I have each seen the greatest works of racial reconciliation happen within the body of Christ, and our hope for furthering the work is found not in faulted humans but in Jesus Christ working in us and through us.

This process of talking, listening, speaking truth, learning to love, confessing wrong ideas, repenting of generational sins, and learning together to be a "chosen race, a royal priesthood, a holy nation, a people for his own possession" (1 Peter 2:9) is a major undertaking. It's easy to lose hope. It's easy to let down our guard and leave an opening for God's enemy to create division and despair. It's easy to be distracted by political agendas and differences that have nothing to do with skin color or ethnicity. It's easy to convince ourselves that we've already done enough just by not hating other people.

We were saved not only to not participate in ugly things but to do the work of reconciliation, healing, and speaking truth with love.

The Apostle Paul tells us that we were saved by grace as a gift from God through Jesus Christ. We are saved *from* our sin, but we are saved *for* a purpose. "For we are his workmanship, created in Christ Jesus for good works, which God prepared beforehand, that we should walk in them" (Ephesians 2:10). It's good to rely on the power of Jesus to refrain from hatred, racism, violence, and ethnically motivated sin, but we were saved not only to *not* participate in ugly things but to *do* the work of reconciliation, healing, and speaking truth with love.

After feeling called to write this book, I faced a time when the fear of writing "as a white person" nearly paralyzed me. What if I say wrong things? What if people attack me for even engaging in this conversation? What if I make things worse? What if I go out on a limb and the book doesn't even make a difference? What if, what if, what if?

God met me in that panic and confronted my fear-based thinking.

There is no room in love for fear. I love my brothers and sisters of all colors. God designed me white, and he designed Saundra black. We both need to embrace our design and also love the other.

I love Jesus Christ. I am called to write. I was committed to the project. I could not let fear restrain me from participating, even if in only a small way, in the work of Christ, the ministry of reconciliation. I long to be where Jesus is at work, and he is at work here, in our midst, underneath the noise, the rhetoric, and the headlines, quietly creating peace from pew to pew, family to family, congregation to congregation, community to community.

Originally, I thought I knew where this project would lead, but God surprised me at every turn. Whereas the noise of the world in discussions on racism leaves me worn out, exhausted, and wondering if we'll ever get anywhere, God's Word and the whispers of his Holy Spirit restore my hope and renew my joy in the work. It is, after all, in its essence just about putting flesh on Jesus's words. This work of reconciliation is just to "love the Lord your God with all your heart and with all your soul and with all your mind," and to "love your neighbor as yourself" (Matthew 22:37, 39). To love is to listen. To love is to help heal. To love is to be genuinely curious and compassionate about another's experiences. To love is to speak truth. To love is to stand for justice. To love is to lay down one's life for another. And God's commands are for all his children of every color. This is work we do together.

God created us in his image, so we humans are incredible creations. He designed us to walk beside him, to relish work, to rise to a challenge, to long to bring unity, beauty, and peace to chaos. Jesus announced that the kingdom has come. Everywhere that we "put on the whole armor of God, that you may be able to stand against the schemes of the devil" (Ephesians 6:11) we proclaim that kingdom and let his light shine. As Christians, we find our unity kneeling at the cross and taking our stand against "the rulers, against the authorities, against the cosmic powers over this present darkness, against the spiritual forces of evil in the heavenly places" (Ephesians 6:12).

It's important to embrace this work as work that the *whole* body of Christ, his church, is responsible to undertake so that we can share the work and encourage one another in it. We each have a part. Some are called to great leadership in ethnic reconciliation, some to mediation, some to giving; and all are called to faith, prayer, and individually treating others as we would be treated ourselves. Every one of us can begin where we are and take the next step in faith, confident in Christ Jesus's presence with us.

Let me close with the words of an ancient Psalm of Ascent that worshipers would sing together. "Behold, how good and pleasant it is when brothers dwell in unity! It is like the precious oil on the head, running down on the beard, on the beard of Aaron, running down on the collar of his robes! It is like the dew of Hermon, which falls on the mountains of Zion! For there the LORD has commanded the blessing, life forevermore" (Psalm 133). This is what we work for—to access and demonstrate the life and the unity that is ours in Christ Jesus. Amen?

COLORFUL CONVERSATION WITH DR. QUANTRILLA ARD

In recent days, I had hoped and expected a lot more from the church at large. But then I also had to remember that the church is a body of individuals. So at the individual level, if people aren't personally motivated to make change, we will see that mentality reflected in the larger community.

I'm seeing a lot of pushback to proposed change, and I'm not quite sure why. I know the conversations being had on topics of race and social justice are uncomfortable for many. I also know it can be painful to pull off the proverbial scab that exists on the wound that racism is in America. With that said, I'm still left wondering why there's so much hesitancy among Christians—who claim to be a gospel-focused, gospel-centric, freedom-centered group of people—to enter into the hard work, to converse, to even acknowledge these issues. If we are looking at racial reconciliation in terms of freedom and healing, which are two tenets central to the gospel, then freedom is for everyone. I find myself concerned that many Christians aren't engaging in these types of conversations because they're afraid of them and running away.

I am witnessing glimmers of hope. In contrast to the group described above, there are many other Christians who are creating tables where conversations can happen, and I'm so grateful for them. There is a gentleman by the name of Joel Muddamalle, who has created a space for people to have dialogue on his own social media pages. These conversations are not based on his opinion; they are 100 percent biblically based. He presents issues he has come across in Scripture that are relevant to the current climate, and he presents them in a way that disarms people. Often, we can come to these conversations with a lot of baggage. Our preconceived notions and personal preferences can put us on the defensive before the conversation begins. But friends, you can't argue with the Word of God.

This method of engaging others pulled me in because Joel starts at the foot of the cross, where all are on the same level. He crafts every conversation with that context and then brings his points back around to today's message. I have found that when people continuously create tables for conversations to happen, you're going to get people to show up. They may not show up all the time and you may not get a large crowd, but at least those who do show up wanting to engage in conversation have a place where they can do it.

I'm a huge fan of having tools to help on this journey. The Conversation Readiness Assessment is an excellent tool. I get asked all the time, "Where do I begin?" Or I hear statements like, "I'm afraid, because I don't want to say the wrong thing." Rather than forcing individuals to engage without support, this resource allows people to come in at whatever entry point is most comfortable for them. It gives people the opportunity to say, "Okay, this is my lane. I may not be comfortable leading, but I'm definitely comfortable learning." Or "I may not know exactly what I'm supposed to be saying, but I'm definitely comfortable listening." I think this assessment is very purposeful, and I think it will break down a lot of the hesitancy to have the conversations in the first place. That is the barrier I am praying to see eliminated.

DR. QUANTRILLA ARD is a faith-based personal and spiritual development writer with a multidisciplinary background in public health and health psychology. Her ethnicity is African American.

STEP 12: CELEBRATE THE HOPE WE HAVE IN CHRIST FOR UNITY AND PEACE.

The God we serve loved celebrations so much, he wove them into the life of his people from the Old Testament to the New. When we celebrate progress, we encourage more, and we let our light so shine before others that they may see our good works and give glory to our Father who is in heaven (paraphrase Matthew 5:16).

Celebrate differences as the creative variety with which God has blessed the church. Host opportunities for friends, neighbors, or church members to share foods or traditions special to their ethnicity. Gather with congregations different from yours and worship together or, if your congregation is deeply diverse, host a celebration of worship in a local park. Create art together, using every form. Join together for service projects and conclude the work with a great feast and celebration. Advocate for justice together and follow that work with a time of praise and prayer.

Celebration is a powerful tool in this work, *and* it's fun for every age.

Scripture

Read, reread, and if you can, memorize 2 Corinthians 5:11–6:1. After you read it, write it out in your own words. Consider that from the day of Pentecost, the body of Christ was a union in Christ of people of differing tribes, tongues, and nations. This work is not new to the church but ongoing with every generation and every culture. Know that there will be setbacks, hard conversations, and spiritual opposition, but know equally well that we have every reason to hope in Christ as stated in Romans 15:13 and Mark 9:23.

What are some scriptural ways to defend against a loss of hope and heart?

What are some ways people celebrated in the Bible? How can their celebrations inform our celebrations as we mark progress toward the goal of racial healing and reconciliation?

Celebrate that hope often. What is one way you can celebrate this hope now?

Starting Places

- Before planning a celebration, ask people how their family celebrates. What are their traditions, foods, places, rituals, arts, and practices in celebrations large and small? Assume less, ask more. Exercise creativity in celebration. Can different musical traditions be combined? What about together planting trees or various flowers to celebrate God's love of variety?
- Include people of various ethnicities in the leadership and ground-level planning rather than having one group create the idea and "fit the other culture in" once the outline has been created.
- Do you have young people who do spoken word poetry, dance, sculpture, animation, or other artistic expressions? Involve them in contributing to the celebration.
- Create a recipe book from your church incorporating dishes from all ethnicities and interspersed with artwork, poetry, or devotions from a variety of skin colors and ages.
- Celebrate in small ways and frequently. Choose a celebration song to sing regularly or celebrate/highlight forward movement during weekly worship with a moment of praise for our God. Together, read Bible verses that speak to hope at every celebration.

Group Discussion Questions

Chapter One

1. Can you relate to Saundra's and Lori's hesitation to engage in conversations about race? What do you think causes most people to hesitate or avoid these conversations?
2. What have been your past experiences with conversations about race? What have you seen as a result of these conversations?
3. What hopes arise in you when considering conversations aimed at racial healing?
4. What challenges faced the early church regarding race and ethnicity? How did they approach those challenges?
5. What does the parable of the Samaritan say to you about Jesus's thoughts on race?

Chapter Two

1. How do you define racism? What are some examples of racism that you have witnessed or experienced?
2. How do you respond when you are accused of racism? How do others around you respond?
3. What's the difference between racism and cultural insensitivity? What are some examples of each?
4. How can we make it safe for someone to ask questions to get to know us if they're afraid of offending us? What opportunities can we create as a church/community for people of different backgrounds/ethnicities to get to know one another?

5. If we use the Bible as our "mirror," or standard, how do we communicate with people who use other measures?

Chapter Three

1. What stories would you tell if asked to share about being your skin color/ethnicity? What was it like for you growing up? As a teen? When you were a young adult? Now?

2. Why do you think people are afraid to listen to others whose experience is different from their own?

3. What do the young people in your life witness and hear regarding people of different ethnicities? What are some ways you're guiding the young people in your life regarding race and ethnicity? Who were your primary examples in relation to race/ethnicity when you were young?

4. What are the benefits for everyone of really listening to others, of being willing to hear their experiences and stories without shutting them down or invalidating their perspective?

5. What are some Scripture passages about listening? How might they apply to racial healing?

Chapter Four

1. Have you ever thought you had little to contribute to racial healing or that what you have to contribute doesn't matter? What has contributed to these feelings or thoughts? How does this chapter impact your thinking on this topic?

2. How does where we live impact our understanding of ethnicity and/or racial relationships? What are some of the places you've lived? What was the ethnic makeup of these places? What have you witnessed in terms of racial tension?

3. What are your thoughts on "racism that hides underground" or that "lurks in the shadows"? Where have you seen this at work or at church? How do we best shed light on these dark places?

4. Can you relate to losing hope about making progress against racism? What are some ways to combat this potential loss of hope? What does the Bible say about hope and change?

5. What has been your struggle with identity? Do you have a strong cultural or ethnic identity? Why or why not? What is your primary identifier and why? What does the Bible say to you about identity?

Chapter Five

1. What experiences—positive or negative—have you had being identified with a particular group: a school, team, club, vocation, location, or culture? What can you take from that to help make you more loving in this conversation on racial healing?
2. What experiences have you had being in a minority? How did these experiences affect you?
3. How do you best experience love from people outside your immediate family group? What do others do that make you feel loved? What do others do that make you wonder if you're loved?
4. What are some scriptural examples of how God wants us to love others? How did those in the early church express love to people who were different from them?
5. What are some biblical ways we love others that don't always feel like love? What are ways we can love people with "tough love" while communicating that they are valued and heard?

Chapter Six

1. Have you seen the power of boycotts used effectively for good? When and how? Have you seen them used to silence truth? When and how? When did Jesus remain silent, and when did he speak when it came to injustice? What examples can you name?
2. What impact has cancel culture had on your willingness to speak biblical truth in public settings? Tell about a time when you have felt silenced or when you spoke up and then felt invalidated or dismissed. How does this continue to affect you today?

3. How does it impact your view of violent protest to consider it as a result of generational trauma? What does the Bible have to say about the consequences of generational sin?

4. What are your thoughts about racial reconciliation being "optional" or "an elective" for some Christians, while action is "required" of others based on skin color or ethnicity?

5. How does God's picture of the church, each part dependent on the others, impact your thinking about the part you play in resolving racial tensions? What does God mean when he says that if one part of the body suffers, we all suffer, and what does that say about the church today?

Chapter Seven

1. Name some reasons it may either be hard or easy for a person to discuss America's history of slavery. Which is true for you, and why?

2. Are the challenges of Christians who know their ancestors participated in the slave trade different from those who believe their family did not participate or actively worked to end slavery? Explain your answer. How did you learn about the history of slavery in America, and what is your understanding of your family's personal history with slavery?

3. What injustices have you personally experienced or witnessed? What was the result of this injustice in your life? How was the injustice resolved? Where did you see God at work in your experience? What role did other Christians play?

4. In what ways does your life reflect the command of Micah 6:8 that we are to "do justice, to love mercy, and to walk humbly with your God"? In what ways would you like to change to reflect this more?

5. Since sincere Christians of all skin colors may disagree on what justice looks like in any single situation, what are some biblical guidelines for discussing these disagreements? How can we continue to disagree and yet continue to be in relationship and to worship together?

Chapter Eight

1. What is different about the culture and times in which you were raised than it is for children and teens today, especially around the topic of race and ethnicity?

2. Where do the young people in your sphere of influence receive the most education/influence around the topic of race and ethnicity? Church? School? Where is it reflected in the teaching of your church on their level? Are there ways you can fill in those gaps?

3. What role does power have to play in the current discussions/debates about race? How does this contribute to the intensity of the rhetoric? What does the Bible teach about power, and where are we having conversations about God's view of power with the next generation?

4. How do the challenges facing parents of color differ from those of white parents, and how are they the same? How can parents of all colors work together to create greater understanding and cooperation between ethnicities that their children can see?

5. What opportunities exist in your faith community for young people to ask questions, express anger, or discuss their doubts? What outreach is happening for older teens or young adults who may feel disconnected with God or with their community? What are some creative ways you can imagine that your church or community can create these opportunities and welcome young people in for support and biblical perspective on the issues of our times?

Chapter Nine

1. Talk about your history with churches and worship. What experiences have you had with worship services and churches you've attended or visited over the years?

2. What are some nonnegotiable aspects of worship for you? What are areas of preference for you in worship? How do you determine what is nonnegotiable and what is preferential?

3. What considerations does your current church make for cultural expression in worship? Does your current church's worship reflect the demographic of the congregation? The demographic of the community? Why or why not? If your worship is multicultural, how does that impact your life in the community? Does it translate outside the church walls?

4. What are your thoughts on the need of some ethnic communities or language groups to worship separately? What are the advantages or disadvantages for the Christian community and for outreach? In what situations might it be loving and advantageous for a group to have worship that is largely homogenous to one ethnicity or language? What could help prevent the group from becoming exclusive or isolated from the rest of the believing community?

5. What pitfalls exist in seeking to be culturally inclusive in worship? What advantage is there in reflecting a variety of cultural expressions back to God in worship? How does our worship contribute to outreach and proclaiming the gospel in our community?

Chapter Ten

1. What does the Bible say are our weapons against the devil's schemes? How can we apply these to the topic of racial/ethnic relationships? What advantage does Satan have in keeping the body of Christ divided, and how does it benefit the spread of the gospel for the body of Christ to be unified?

2. Have you ever thought or heard someone else say that we should focus on the gospel and that working on ethnic reconciliation may detract energy from that? What are your opinions on that topic? In what ways might social justice/racial reconciliation either contribute or detract from the preaching of the gospel of Jesus Christ?

3. What does it look like to "keep the gospel central" when working through cultural or racial issues? In what ways does racial unity within the church contribute to the spread of the gospel?

4. What spiritual gifts do you have, and how do you exercise them in the church? How does the way you contribute to the body of Christ (whether through preaching, giving, overseeing the nursery, or greeting newcomers) contribute to the work of evangelism?

5. What does it mean to be "part of a body," and how can this biblical teaching be a guide for the church's work toward greater unity? How does it inform our understanding of cultural and racial differences within the body of Christ and what hope does it offer in this conversation?

Chapter Eleven

1. Have you ever been in a conversation about race or ethnicity that became heated or left people with hurt feelings? How has that affected you in relation to engaging in more conversations about this topic?

2. What were some of the ethnic challenges facing the early church? How did they approach them and overcome them?

3. How can it be helpful to build a list of "strengths and agreements" that we refer to frequently during hard conversations? What would be the advantage of discussing guidelines for conversations before they begin? What barriers exist to doing this?

4. What motivates you to overcome your fears of being vulnerable or possibly exposing your own bias in order to engage in hard conversations? What are some guidelines that would help you feel safe about doing this and more confident that the conversation would lead to successful outcomes?

5. Reflect on the three stages Saundra listed—Ready to Listen, Ready to Learn, and Ready to Lead. Where do you believe you are right now? What is your next step? What steps are needed to help you move to the next stage?

Chapter Twelve

1. What fears do you have associated with sharing your perspective on race/ethnicity in America or in your community/church

today? What contributes to the creation of those fears? What biblical truth can contribute to overcoming them?

2. Besides talking, what are ways that people of different cultures, backgrounds, or perspectives can come together and find common ground? What experiences have you had that involved more action than talking, and how did that impact your relationships?

3. Saundra and Lori are writers, so they have used their writing gifts toward the work of racial reconciliation. What are your gifts, skills, talents, or understanding that you might contribute to this work, and how might God use them? What have you been doing so far, and what could you see God doing with you next?

4. Does the work of racial reconciliation exhaust you or the idea of it wear you out? What biblical truths can help you hold onto hope in the face of such a large and complex topic? How do you combat the fatigue caused by the "noise of the world" and continue making progress even if it's in small increments? How do we not give up?

5. How do you celebrate? How does your church celebrate? What opportunities are there in the life of your faith community for celebration, and how can these celebrations reflect the cultures of all who worship with you? What can you celebrate about the work God is doing in our midst to bring brothers and sisters of different ethnicities together for our good and for his glory?

Acknowledgments

Saundra

This book exists because of Lori's courage to ask a casual acquaintance to have a conversation about racial reconciliation. Thank you for the invitation to join you on this journey and for your willingness to have hard conversations.

Bobby, Tristan, and Isaiah, you are my faithful support system. You guys cheer me on to be better every day and to wholeheartedly follow God. Thank you for your grace during long writing sessions and for your enduring love.

George and Sallie Dalton, thank you for your unwavering support. You keep me mindful of the importance of showing love through both the big and the small acts of caring.

Bob Hostetler, your encouragement and prayers are more than I could ask for in a literary agent. I am deeply thankful for your guidance.

Finally, I want to thank all of the voices contributing to the conversations within this book: Jo Saxton, Maria Gill, Jamie Ivey, Patricia Raybon, Dorina Lazo Gilmore-Young, Glynnis Whitwer, Dr. Quantrilla Ard, Kent Mattox, Dr. Derwin Gray, Rev. Doug Stevens, Vivian Mabuni, and Rachel Kang. Your input has been invaluable.

Lori

Thank you, Saundra, for the mercy, grace, and excellence you brought to this project. What a joy it is to know you and work beside you in the kingdom.

To my ever-expanding family—Rob, Zack, Jessica, Christian, Logan, Hannah, Andrew, and Sam ("Little Chief"), you contribute to my writing in countless ways, but more than that, you are my beating heart.

Bob Hostetler, you are a writer's agent. Your prayers fuel the fire in my heart when the enemy tries to dampen my hopes. Thank you for kneeling beside us.

To my church family at First Baptist Church in Hope Valley—your faith in Christ, your love for one another, and your commitment to represent Jesus inspire me every day.

To Steve Barclift, a huge thank you! You have encouraged my work all along. To the entire team at Kregel, thank you for your work in making this book shine and in partnering with us in sharing this message.

And to all who came before us, thank you for the progress you've made in this work. To those who labor beside us, thank you for being part of the solution. And to those who come after us, may you make the progress that to us is now only the dream for which we pray, in Jesus's name. Amen.

Notes

How to Get the Most from This Book

1. A. J. Austin, W. T. Cox, P. G. Devine, and P. S. Forscher, "Long-term Reduction in Implicit Race Bias: A Prejudice Habit-breaking Intervention." *Journal of Experimental Social Psychology* 48, no. 6 (2012), 1267–1278.

Chapter Two

1. John Root, "Issues for the Church in a Multi-Racial Society," *Themelios* 10, no. 2 (1985), accessed December 17, 2021, https://www.thegospelcoalition.org /themelios/article/issues-for-the-church-in-a-multi-racial-society/.

Chapter Three

1. "First Impressions," *Psychology Today*, accessed December 17, 2021, https:// www.psychologytoday.com/us/basics/first-impressions.
2. Angela Oswalt Morelli, MSW; Mark Dombeck, Ph.D., ed., "Prejudice," *Gracepoint*, accessed December 17, 2021, https://www.gracepointwellness .org/1262-child-development-parenting-middle-8-11/article/38395-prejudice.

Chapter Four

1. Timothy Keller, "The Healing of Anger," Gospel in Life, August 10, 2015, YouTube video, 40:15, https://www.youtube.com/watch?v=2v-2ewGCQB4.
2. Andrea Brandt, PhD, M.F.T., "Is Your Anger a Cover for Shame," *Psychology Today*, July 5, 2016, https://www.psychologytoday.com/us/blog /mindful-anger/201607/is-your-anger-cover-shame.

Chapter Six

1. Kate Becker, "When Computers Were Human: The Black Women Behind NASA's Success," *NewScientist*, January 20, 2017, https://www.newscien tist.com/article/2118526-when-computers-were-human-the-black-women -behind-nasas-success/#ixzz6sPnbPDMt.

Chapter Seven

1. "First Enslaved Africans Arrive in Jamestown, Setting the Stage for Slavery in North America," History.com, August 13, 2019, https://www.history.com/this-day-in-history/first-african-slave-ship-arrives-jamestown-colony.
2. Latasha Morrison, *Be the Bridge: Pursuing God's Heart for Racial Reconciliation* (Waterbrook, 2019), 34.
3. Timothy Keller, "Justice in the Bible," *Life in the Gospel*, September 2020, https://quarterly.gospelinlife.com/justice-in-the-bible/.

Chapter Eight

1. B. Kennedy, "Repentance," *The Lexham Bible Dictionary*, ed. J. D. Barry, D. Bomar, D. R. Brown, R. Klippenstein, D. Mangum, C. Sinclair Wolcott, and W. Widder (Bellingham, WA: Lexham Press, 2016).

Chapter Nine

1. Martin Luther King, Jr. "Advice for Living," The Martin Luther King, Jr. Research and Education Institute, accessed January 5, 2022, https://kinginstitute.stanford.edu/king-papers/documents/advice-living-5.
2. Nadra Kareem Nittle, "5 Ways to Make Your Racially Segregated Church More Diverse," ThoughtCo., April 30, 2019, https://www.thoughtco.com/diversify-your-racially-segregated-church-2834542.
3. Charles R. Foster and Theodore Brelsford, *We Are the Church Together: Cultural Diversity in Congregational Life* (Harrisburg, PA: Trinity Press International, 1996).
4. Tom Gjelten, "Multiracial Congregations May Not Bridge Racial Divide," NPR, July 17, 2020, https://www.npr.org/2020/07/17/891600067/multiracial-congregations-may-not-bridge-racial-divide.

Chapter Ten

1. Priscilla Shirer, "Going Beyond Ministries with Priscilla Shirer - The Armor," Going Beyond Ministries, August 31, 2017, YouTube video, https://www.youtube.com/watch?v=ePbAv6NuKzQ.
2. "What is a Kinsman-Redeemer?" Common Bible Questions, Bibleinfo.com, accessed March 17, 2022, https://www.bibleinfo.com/en/questions/what-is-a-kinsman-redeemer.

Chapter Twelve

1. For more information, visit "Freedom Riders," History.com, updated January 20, 2022, https://www.history.com/topics/black-history/freedom-rides.

Recommended Resources

The Art of Hard Conversations: Biblical Tools for the Tough Talks That Matter by Lori Stanley Roeleveld. Grand Rapids: Kregel Publications, 2019

Be the Bridge: Pursuing God's Heart for Racial Reconciliation by Latasha Morrison. Colorado Springs: WaterBrook, 2019

Building a Multiethnic Church: A Gospel Vision of Love, Grace, and Reconciliation in a Divided World by Derwin L. Gray and foreword by Matt Chandler. Nashville: Thomas Nelson, 2021

The Listening Life: Embracing Attentiveness in a World of Distraction by Adam S. McHugh. Westmont, IL: IVP Books, 2015

Reading While Black: African American Biblical Interpretation as an Exercise in Hope by Esau McCaulley. Westmont, IL: IVP Academic, 2020

The Third Option: Hope for a Racially Divided Nation by Miles McPherson and foreword by Drew Brees. Brentwood, TN: Howard Books, 2018

Discover how your next conversation could impact someone's life forever– maybe even your own.

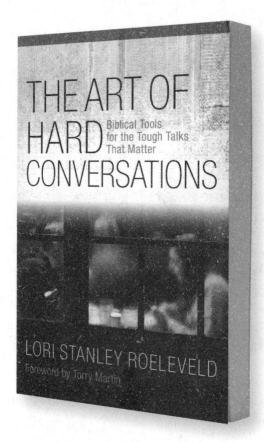

"Lori writes as a coach and a confidant, gently encouraging both the bold and the bashful to approach hard conversations with finesse and grace."

—Lynn H. Blackburn, best-selling and award-winning author